Guide to Ancient Rome

Texts by
Ada Gabucci

Photographs by
Giovanni Rinaldi

Electa

Contents

The Valley of the Colosseum

"As long as the Colosseum stands Rome shall stand. When the Colosseum falls Rome shall fall with it." So wrote the Venerable Bede in the eighth century. Until the nineteenth century the open space now named Piazza del Colosseo was a valley ringed round with five hills, the Palatine, Velia, Fagutal, Oppian and Caelius. In antiquity the area was originally occupied by houses; but in 64 AD the Emperor Nero took it in hand. After a fire ravaged the hillsides he incorporated it into the construction of his immense and sumptuous palace, significantly named the Domus Aurea or Golden House (p. 18).

At the entrance to the Domus Aurea stood a gigantic bronze statue, 32 metres high, of Nero as the Sun God, an imitation of the celebrated Colossus of Rhodes (ill. 5 and 136). The statue was spared by Vespasian, though he demolished all other traces of his predecessor's megalomania. Vespasian restored the valley to public use and began to work on the amphitheatre called the Colosseum after Nero's colossal statue (p. 8).

In about 80 AD a monumental fountain (ill. 2) stood in the area now in front of the Arch of Constantine, a later work (p. 14). The water gushed out of a cone 17 metres high into a basin 16 metres across. Its shape, rather like the conical pillars that marked the turn in the chariot races (p. 42), with the water pouring down its sides earned it the name of the Meta Sudans or Sweating Pillar.

The present state of Piazza del Colosseo is the result of demolition work in the 1930s to create the Via dell'Imperio and Via dei Trionfi (now Via dei Fori Imperiali and Via di San Gregorio). This entailed the levelling of the Velia and destruction of the last imposing remains of the Meta Sudans and the base of Nero's Colossus.

1. *Detail of the Colosseum in a watercolour by L.J. Duc (1802–1879). Ecole des Beaux-Arts, Paris.*
2. *The Arch of Constantine and the Meta Sudans seen from the Colosseum (conjectural reconstruction and present state).*
3. *The Colosseum.*

◀4 5▲ 6▼

THE COLOSSEUM

Construction of the Colosseum as an arena for public shows was begun by the Emperor Vespasian and completed by his son Titus. He inaugurated it in 80 AD with games (p. 12) lasting for a hundred days, at which 5000 wild animals were slain.

Under the empire the Colosseum was extensively repaired a number of times following fires and earthquakes. On 23 August, 217 AD it was repeatedly struck by lightning and all the wooden structures, which included the floor of the arena, went up in the blaze. The city's seven fire-fighting battalions and sailors from the fleet at Misenus failed to quell the flames. The Colosseum remained unserviceable for some years but in 223 the Emperor Alexander Severus restored it to its ancient splendour. Despite the efforts of Constantine and his successors to abolish gladiatorial combats they were finally banned only in 404 by Honorius. For over a century thereafter the only entertainments were combats with wild animals (p. 12). The last spectacle was presented in 523.

4. *Vespasian (68–79 AD). Rome, Museo Nazionale Romano.*
5. *The Colosseum: detail of a model. Museo della Civiltà Romana, Rome.*
6. *The Colosseum and the Arch of Constantine in a painting by Canaletto (1697–1768). Paul Getty Museum, Malibu.*

History of the Excavations

The loss of the Colosseum's original function as an arena led to its progressive decay and alteration. It was stripped of its metal fittings and the stone was carted away for reuse as building material. But the edifice was never completely abandoned: between the twelfth and thirteenth centuries it was incorporated into the fortress of the Frangipane family, and in the sixteenth century the arena was consecrated and a chapel built on it.

In the seventeenth and eighteenth centuries greater interest in preserving relics of the past led to a ban on the removal of stone for building material. The first systematic excavations began in the nineteenth century and revealed the structures below the arena. There was extensive restoration.

Since then scholars have explored the Colosseum systematically and there is currently an imposing program of archaeological studies, restoration and defence of the monument.

◄7   8▲

7. *Coin from the reign of Titus depicting the Colosseum and the Meta Sudans. Museo Nazionale Romano (Palazzo Massimo alle Terme), Rome.*
8. *Excavations in the Colosseum in a painting by H. Robert (1733–1808). Prado, Madrid.*

The Interior of the Colosseum

Sixty-six numbered entrances led to the three tiers of seating. The amphitheatre could be covered by an immense awning hoisted by a squad of sailors from the fleet at Misenus. At the two sides of the smaller axis of the arena there were honorary stands for the emperor, consuls, Vestal Virgins (p. 56), and other court dignitaries. The topmost tier of the amphitheatre provided standing room for the humblest classes.

The arena itself was an oval measuring 86 meters across its longer axis. Its surface was a deck of wooden boards covering a dense network of tunnels which contained the scenery, hoists and pens for wild animals. The Colosseum could comfortably hold a crowd of 50,000 (like a medium-sized football stadium today) and the spectacles lasted several hours.

9 ▲   10 ▼

11 ▲

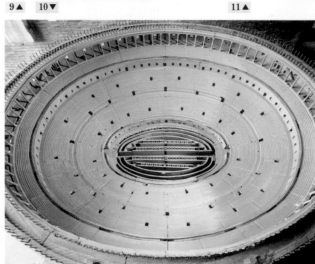

9. *The inner arches.*
10. *The Colosseum, model. Museo della Civiltà Romana, Rome.*
11. *Stone block to which the awning was moored.*
12. *The upper terrace.*
13. *Cross-section of the cavea and system of entrances and exits.*
14. *Gladiator. Detail of a mosaic (fifth century AD). Galleria Borghese, Rome.*
15. *Interior of the Colosseum.*

12 ▼

13 ▼

14 ▲   15 ▶

WILD BEASTS AND GLADIATORS

Professional gladiators were very popular. They might be free men or slaves (who sometimes won their freedom by their victories in the arena) and they were named according to their weapons. The *retiarius*, armed with net and trident, fought against the *mirmillo*, so called after the fish (*murma*) that decorated his helmet. Their combat symbolised the struggle between fisherman and fish. The "Samnites" were armed with a heavy sword and rectangular shield, while the "Thracians" fought with a short sword and small round shield. In provincial towns a vanquished combatant was rarely put to death: it took years to train a good gladiator and the impresario who mounted the games lost heavily by it. But in Rome, where the games were put on by the emperors, expense was no object and the public spared the loser only in exceptional circumstances. Combats were also organised between criminals sentenced to death. In this case clemency was never shown: a swordsman who survived a series of gruelling combats would be dispatched by a fresh gladiator sent into the ring expressly for the purpose. Gladiatorial combats were not the only entertainment: there were also wild-animal hunts, fights between wild beasts, or even exhibitions of trained animals without bloodshed. The public reacted with admiration and excitement to the exotic animals and the sudden appearance of natural scenery and backdrops from which emerged fierce beasts and huntsmen.

16. *Scene of combat in a wall painting (fourth century AD). Museo Archeologico Nazionale, Paestum.*
17. *Helmet of a gladiator with scenes of the fall of Troy (70–79 AD). Museo Archeologico Nazionale Rome, Naples.*
18. *The Ludus Magnus, one of the four barracks that supplied the Colosseum with gladiators. There were also storehouses and hospitals connected with the games.*
19–20. *Games in the Circus and gladiators with a bull, deer and ostrich in mosaics in a villa near Tusculum (fifth century AD). Galleria Borghese, Rome.*
21. *Gladiators in a fourth-century mosaic. Archaeological Museum, Madrid.*

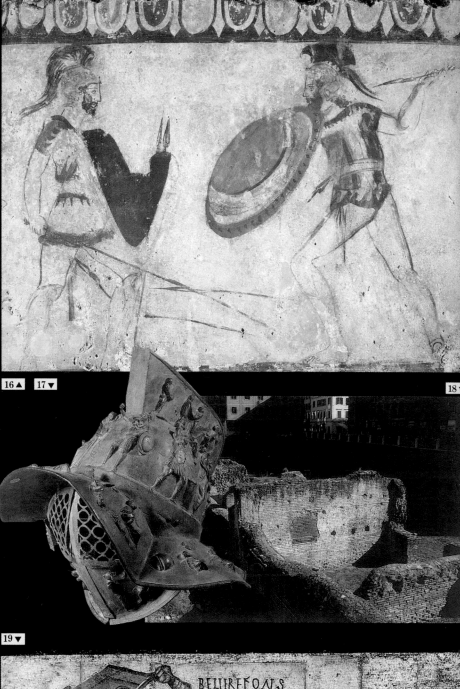

16▲ 17▼ 18▼

19▼

THE ARCH OF CONSTANTINE

After defeating his rival Maxentius at the Battle of the Milvian Bridge (28 October 312) Constantine moved his residence to Trier in Germany. He only returned to Rome three years later to celebrate the tenth anniversary of his ascent to power. He inaugurated the arch that the Senate had erected in his honour on the long processional route followed by generals awarded a triumph: it ran from the Field of Mars through the city to the Temple of Capitoline Jove.

Since there was little time to complete the immense structure the Senate took the unprecedented step of reusing parts of earlier monuments, especially public buildings from the reigns of Trajan, Hadrian, and Marcus Aurelius. Four panels from the reign of Trajan were taken from the attic of the Basilica Ulpia (p. 68), while the tondos of Hadrian probably came from the entrance to a shrine dedicated to Antinous, Hadrian's young favourite. The carvings of Marcus Aurelius probably came from a triumphal arch celebrating his victories in Germany. For the sake of uniformity the faces of the emperors were all recarved to represent Constantine.

22 ▲ 23 ►

24 ▼

22. *View of the south side.*
23. *Head of the colossal statue of Constantine (306–337 AD). Musei Capitolini, Rome.*
24. *Drawing of the Arch of Constantine showing the periods from which the carvings date:*

   reign of Trajan
   reign of Hadrian
   reign of Marcus Aurelius
   reign of Constantine

25. *Tondo with a sacrifice to Diana from the reign of Hadrian.*

25 ▼

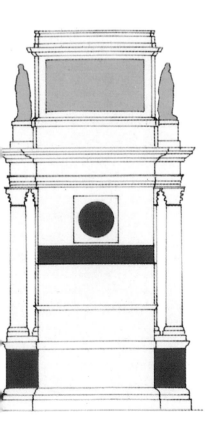

Carvings on the Arch of Constantine

"To the Emperor Caesar Flavius Constantinus Maximus Pius Felix Augustus, the Senate and People of Rome dedicated an arch decorated with scenes of triumph, since by divine inspiration and great wisdom with his army and righteous weapons he liberated the state from tyranny and all faction."

The inscription on the front of the arch represents Constantine as the restorer of the Empire, guided by divinity. The wars and triumphs of great emperors of the past cast an aura of legitimacy round his power and provided the political consensus needed for maintaining a stable government.

The great storied frieze running along the middle of the smaller sides of the arch and above the side-openings represents the Emperor's feats: his departure from Milan; the siege of Verona, where he is crowned by a winged Victory; the defeat of Maxentius at the Milvian bridge; his entry into Rome; his speech to the population and a distribution of money. In the last two scenes Constantine appears in the middle of the composition, disproportionately larger than the other figures, ranged symmetrically on either side and facing him, clearly indicating their subordination.

28 ▲   29 ▼

26–27. Statues of Dacian prisoners from the reign of Trajan and reliefs from the reign of Marcus Aurelius with scenes from the German campaigns: a barbarian chief presented to the Romans; presentation of prisoners to the Emperor; speech of the sovereign to his soldiers; a sacrifice in the camp.
28–29. Tondos from the reign of Hadrian: departure for a hunt and (below) hunting scene.
30. Reliefs on the north front, drawing.
31. Winged Victory, relief from the reign of Constantine.

THE VALLEY OF THE COLOSSEUM

30 ▼

31 ▶

VOTIS · X.

VOTIS · XX.

IMP · CAES · FL · CONSTANTINO · MAXIMO
P · F · AVGVSTO · S · P · Q · R ·
QVOD · INSTINCTV · DIVINITATIS · MENTIS
MAGNITVDINE · CVM · EXERCITV · SVO
TAM · DE · TYRANNO · QVAM · DE · OMNI · EIVS
FACTIONE · VNO · TEMPORE · IVSTIS
REM · PVBLICAM · VLTVS · EST · ARMIS
ARCVM · TRIVMPHIS · INSIGNEM · DICAVIT

THE DOMUS AUREA

Immediately after the fire of 64 AD, which destroyed most of the centre of Rome, Nero built a new imperial residence. This was far bigger and more luxurious than the previous one, the Domus Transitoria (p. 28). Its walls were decked with gold and precious stones, giving it the name the Domus Aurea or Golden House. Designed by the architects Severus and Celeres, the new palace was immense: it covered the Palatine, Velia and Oppian hills and the valley where the Colosseum was later built. "Buildings the size of towns" surrounded a pool almost as big as a sea and behind them rose "villas with fields, vineyards and pastures, woods swarming with all sorts of creatures, wild and domestic." No less remarkable was the luxury of the ornaments, for we are told that "the dining rooms had ceilings sheathed with movable plates of ivory and with apertures through which flowers and perfumes could be poured." Of the Domus Aurea there now remains a single pavilion on the Oppian, preserved because it was incorporated into the Baths of Trajan built above it (p. 109). All memory of the palace was lost during the later Empire and Middle Ages. In the late fifteenth century it was rediscovered by artists and antiquarians, who descended into the underground grottoes filled with earth and there copied the decorations in the vaulting. This gave rise to the new genre of decoration called "grotesque." Some of these chambers, made famous by drawings and engravings published in the eighteenth century, are now open to the public. They include "the corridor of the eagles," the nympheaum of Ulysses and Polyphemus, the monumental octagonal chamber, a room with a gilded vault, the chamber of Achilles at Scyros, and the chamber of Hector and Andromache.

32. *Reconstruction of the great hall of the Domus Aurea with the Laocoön, in a painting by G. Chedanne (nineteenth century). Musée des Beaux-Arts, Rouen.*
33. *View of the octagonal chamber of the pavilion on the Oppian.*
34. *Scene at the centre of the vault in the Room of Achilles at Scyros.*
35. *Painted friezes in the vault of the room of Hector and Andromache.*
36. *Nero. Museo Palatino, Rome.*

32 ▲   33 ▼

34▲ 35▼

36 ▶

The Palatine

According to Varro (116–27 BC), a celebrated scholar of Roman antiquities, Rome was founded on the Palatine in 754 BC by Romulus, who traced a furrow with a plough to mark its confines. His account may be rather fanciful, but the Palatine was certainly the site of the earliest Latin settlement on the banks of the Tiber and also the nucleus of the Eternal City. Some very primitive religious traditions were connected with the Palatine. One was the feast of the *Lupercalia*, connected with the she-wolf, Rome's sacred animal, when wolf-priests clothed in goatskins ran about the hill whipping all who chanced within reach. Throughout the republican period new cults were introduced to the Palatine and numerous temples erected. The hill eventually became the residence of the Roman ruling class and here Augustus was born. This was important for the hill's future because as emperor he fixed his residence on the hill and began to construct the Imperial Palaces.

In the following century an immense palace complex grew up on the Palatine and was frequently altered and extended till, by the end of the imperial period, it sprawled across the whole hill. The Latin name of the hill, *Palatium*, became synonymous with the emperor's palace and with this significance it eventually entered the various European languages.

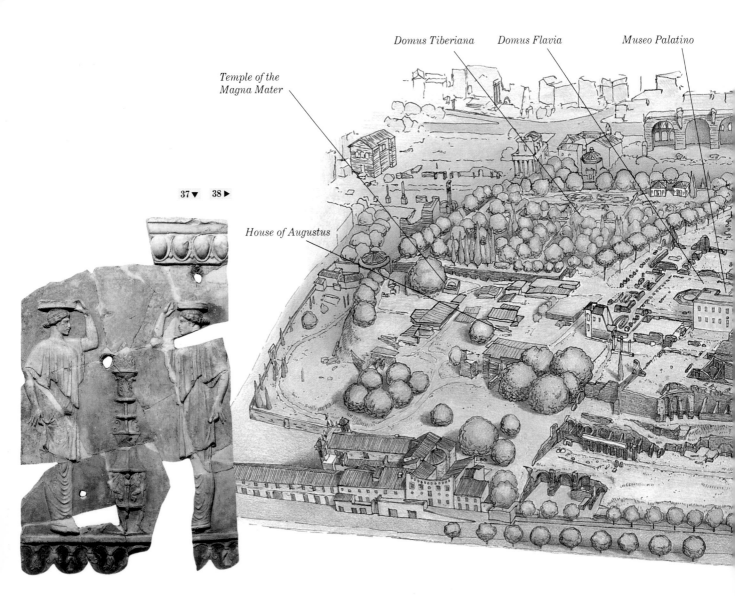

Domus Tiberiana   Domus Flavia   Museo Palatino

Temple of the
Magna Mater

37 ▼   38 ▶

House of Augustus

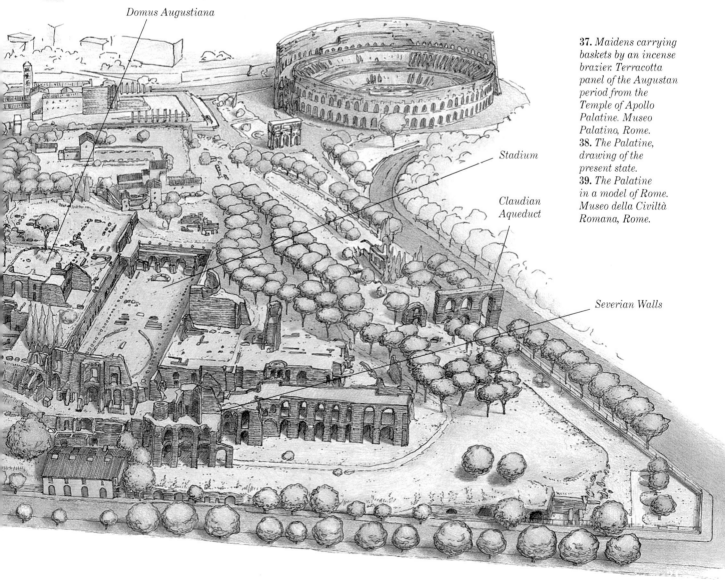

Domus Augustiana

Stadium

Claudian
Aqueduct

Severian Walls

37. *Maidens carrying baskets by an incense brazier. Terracotta panel of the Augustan period from the Temple of Apollo Palatine. Museo Palatino, Rome.*
38. *The Palatine, drawing of the present state.*
39. *The Palatine in a model of Rome. Museo della Civiltà Romana, Rome.*

THE PALATINE

The German poet Johann Wolfgang Goethe (1749–1832) described the impressions aroused by the sight of the Palatine: "In the evening, after taking a leisurely view of all these beautiful things, we went to the Palatine gardens. The spaces between the ruins and the imperial palaces have been made fertile and attractive by beds of flowers. We enjoyed a splendid evening congenial to our taste high up on an open terrace shaded by magnificent trees and surrounded by fragments of ornate capitals, smooth and fluted columns, shattered carvings and similar remains, as elsewhere there might be tables chairs and benches for some cheerful outdoor gathering. When, at the hour of sunset, we contemplated that rich and varied panorama with eyes wide-open and long practised, we had to confess that such a picture could still be admired even after all those that we had viewed during the day."

40 ▲   41 ▼

40. *The Palatine (conjectural reconstruction and present state).*
41. *Two views of the Palatine at sunset.*
42. *The Palatine in a drawing by G.B. Piranesi (1720–1778).*

41 ▼   42 ▲

The Temple of the Magna Mater

The cult of the Magna Mater (Great Mother) Cybele was introduced to Rome in 204 BC, during a difficult period of Roman history: for almost fifteen years the city had been engaged in warfare with the Carthaginian general Hannibal. As part of the intense religious activity designed to curry favour with the gods, the Senate consulted the Sibylline books, a collection of prophecies, probably of Greek origin, traditionally believed to have been brought to Rome by Tarquin the Proud.

The simulacrum of the goddess, a black stone, perhaps a meteorite, shaped like an elongated cone, was removed from the sanctuary at Pessinus in Asia Minor and shipped to Rome, where it was kept in the Temple of Victory on the Palatine until a special shrine could be erected to the goddess.

The Temple of the Magna Mater was inaugurated in 191 BC with the *Ludi Megalenses*, a series of festivities for which Plautus and Terence wrote some of their finest comedies. The festival was repeated from 4–10 April every year to mark the arrival of the cult of Cybele in Rome.

43 ▲   44 ▶

43. *Remains of the temple of the Magna Mater.*
44. *The Magna Mater enthroned, from the Antonine period.*
45. *Axonometric reconstruction of the Temples of the Magna Mater and of Victory.*
46. *Outline of the ruins on the Palatine and imaginary reconstruction of the ancient buildings in a watercolour by J.J. Clerget (1808–1877). Ecole des Beaux-Arts, Paris.*

45 ▲   46 ▼

24

The Temple of Apollo

In 36 BC Augustus decided to erect a temple to Apollo after the battle of Naulochos against Sextus Pompey and it was completed eight years later. The edifice formed part of the public section of Augustus's residence (p. 26), with which it was closely connected. The temple was made entirely of Luna marble (now called Carrara marble) and housed the cult statues of Apollo, Diana and Latona, the work of famous Greek sculptors four centuries earlier. The *Sibylline Books*, kept in golden cases, were carefully stored in the base of the statue of Apollo.

The temple faced onto the Portico of the Danaides, so-called because it contained statues of the mythical daughters of King Danaus of Egypt (ill. 79). The temple may have been decorated with the splendid polychrome terracotta panels found on the site and now exhibited in the Museo Palatino (p. 38). Of the whole complex today it is only possible to visit the nucleus inside the walls, made of concrete, now stripped of its tufa cladding and with traces of marble floors and fragments of columns and capitals.

47 ▲

47. Athene, Perseus and the Gorgon in a terracotta panel from the Augustan period from the Temple of Apollo Palatine. Museo Palatino, Rome.
48. The ruins of the Temple of Apollo.

46 ▼   **48** ▲

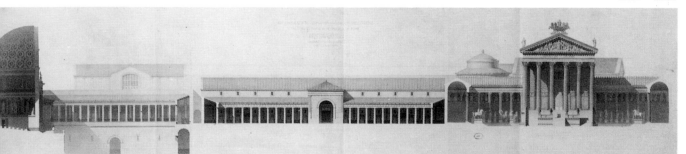

The House of Augustus

Suetonius, a Roman historian and man of letters, has left a description of the house of Augustus on a site east of the Temple of the Magna Mater (p. 24). "He moved to the Palatine, but again into a modest house that had belonged to Hortensius. It was neither large nor luxurious. Outside it had only short porticoes with columns of Alban stone and the rooms were not floored with marble or mosaics of particular artistic value. For over forty years he slept, summer and winter, in the same bedroom." On returning to Rome in 36 BC, after defeating Sextus Pompey at Naulochos, Augustus bought up the adjoining buildings to create a complex consisting of his private home, which still stands, the Temple of Apollo and an official residence for public functions. The residence was later incorporated into the palace of the Emperor Domitian, thereafter called the Domus Augustiana (p. 34).

49. *Statue of Augustus from the Via Labicana. This portrait depicts Augustus, perhaps posthumously, as Pontifex Maximus or High Priest, a title he took in 12 BC. Museo Nazionale Romano (Palazzo Massimo alle Terme), Rome.*
50. *Frescoes in the Room of Masks in the House of Augustus, from about 30 BC.*
51. *Frescoes in the House of Livia, also from about 30 BC.*

◄49   50▲   51▼

52 ▲

52. *The House of Livia and the House of Augustus.*
53. *Portrait conjectured to be of Livia, first century
BC. Musei Capitolini, Rome.*
54. *The Palace of the Caesars on the Palatine
in a watercolour by F. Dutert (1845–1905).
Ecole des Beaux-Arts, Paris.*

53 ▶

54 ▼

FRESCOES
OF THE PALATINE

Frescoes were the commonest form of wall decoration in ancient Rome. The colours were ground up in water and applied directly to the wet surface, usually several layers of plaster which were slow to dry and so enabled a large area to be covered with paintings. The Room of Masks in the House of Augustus has a fairly complex decorative scheme. In what is known as the "second Pompeian style," the walls seem to open out into *trompe l'oeil* vistas between architectural motifs typical of stage painting. The theatrical theme is continued in the masks decorating the cornices painted on the walls. In the middle of each wall appears a painting of a rural shrine. This seems to be the bedroom where Augustus slept for over forty years, while the adjoining room, decorated with festoons of pine fronds between slender pillars, may be the Empress Livia's bedroom. The frescoes of the room known as the Aula Isiaca represent a late phase of the "second Pompeian style." They exemplify the fashion for Egyptian art which influenced Roman painting between the period when Caesar brought Cleopatra to Rome and the aftermath of the battle of Actium (31 BC), culminating in the death of the celebrated Queen. The paintings from a room below the basilica of the Domus Flavia (p. 32), now in a Renaissance loggia close by the Museo Palatino (p. 38) depict myths of the Egyptian goddess Isis and her cult symbols. The whole of the pictorial decoration of the Aula Isiaca, now partly lost but reconstructed from drawings and watercolours made in the eighteenth century when the room was rediscovered, is a clear profession of faith in the Egyptian deities. The richness and refinement of the frescoes and stuccos, enhanced by generous gilding, show this chamber was part of a rich and imposing Palatine dwelling. The Domus Transitoria was Nero's first home. It linked the buildings erected on the Palatine by his predecessors with the imperial buildings on the Esquiline. Only a few chambers and some of the decorations still survive: the rest was burned down in the terrible fire which destroyed half the buildings of Rome on the night of 19 July, 64 AD.

55. *Room of the Masks in the House of Augustus.*
56. *Frescoes in the House of Livia.*
57. *Augustus's study, reconstructed in 1990, in his house on the Palatine.*
58–59. *Frescoes in the Aula Isiaca dating from 30–20 BC.*
60. *Fragment of wall decorations in the Domus Transitoria, mid-first century AD. Museo Palatine, Rome.*

55 ▲   56 ▼

57 ▼

58 ▲   59 ▼

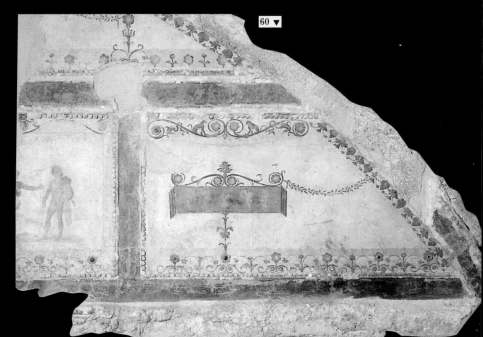

60 ▼

◀ 61

62 ▶

The Domus Tiberiana

The complex built by Tiberius on the Palatine covered much of the west side of the hill between the Temple of the Great Mother (p. 24) and the hillside towards the forum, perhaps the site of the emperor's paternal home. The buildings are little known, as the area was covered in the sixteenth century by the Garden of the Farnese family, in part still existing, and so excavations have only explored their edges.

We know that the residence of Tiberius was enlarged by Caligula and restored by Domitian, Hadrian and Septimius Severus. It long remained in use as the residence of the designated heir to the empire, while the reigning emperor occupied the nearby Domus Augustiana (p. 34). For example Marcus Aurelius and Lucius Verus both moved here after their adoption by the Emperor Antoninus Pius.

61. *Sardonyx cameo with the bust of Tiberius from the first half of the first century AD. Kunsthistorisches Museum, Vienna.*
62. *The Domus Tiberiana.*
63. *Aphrodite, from the Domus Tiberiana (late first century BC). Museo Palatino, Rome.*

THE PALATINE

The Domus Flavia

The Emperor Domitian, like his predecessors, established his residence and court on the Palatine. The great palace, inaugurated in 92 AD, had two entrances, one to the state rooms (the Domus Flavia) and one to the private apartments (the Domus Augustiana, p. 34). The official part of the building was laid out around a large porticoed court with various reception rooms ranged round it. In particular a splendid state room, called the Aula Regia, decorated with niches set between columns, served as the audience chamber. Here the throne was placed in the middle of an apse (a semicircular wall forming a recess). At the side of the throne room there was a basilica (p. 44), its interior divided in three by two rows of columns, and a building (the *lararium*) where the images of members of the royal family were placed after their deaths. On the opposite side of the courtyard stood the great triclinium or banqueting hall flanked by two smaller rooms at the centre of which were two oval fountains (nymphaeums). The playing of the waters could be admired by the banqueters through the great windows between the triclinium and the side chambers. Hadrian installed a heating system in the banqueting hall so that it could be used in winter. The marble pavement still visible was part of restoration work under Maxentius.

Domitian's palace aroused the admiration of his contemporaries by its splendour and the immense size of the lofty chambers, probably decorated with marble and richly furnished. The grandeur of the architecture and the natural setting of the palace created the impression that it was truly the dwelling of a *dominus et deus*, a god ruling over the earth.

◄ 64   65 ▲

66 ▲   67 ►

64. *Domitian (81–96 AD). Musei Capitolini, Rome.*
65. *Section through the Domus Flavia (conjectural) in a watercolour by F. Dutert (1845–1905).*
66. *The Domus Flavia (conjectural reconstruction and present state).*
67. *One of the nymphaeums of the Domus Flavia.*

The Domus Augustiana

The private wing of the Palace of Domitian, called the Domus Augustiana because it incorporated Augustus's official residence, was built on two levels to contain the slope of the Palatine Hill. Its curving facade with the main entrance faced the Circus Maximus (p. 40). On entering from this side, one passed through the outer chambers and came to an inner court surrounded by columns (called a peristyle). This was largely occupied by a monumental fountain decorated with a pattern formed by four *peltae*, shields shaped like half-moons legendarily used by the Amazons. Round this courtyard were ranged symmetrically the rooms of the house of Domitian, set on two floors and with vaulted ceilings. A staircase led to the upper floor, the official residence, where a second peristyle was decorated with a large pool with a little island in the middle, on which stood a temple, perhaps to Minerva. The emperor probably only occupied the rooms on the upper floor, recognisable by their complex layout and small size.

◄ 68   69▲   70▼

THE PALATINE

34

68. *Dancer from the age of Hadrian in the Domus Augustiana. Museo Palatino, Rome.*
69–70. *Peristyle of the Domus Augustiana.*

71. *Drawing of the present state of the Domus Augustiana.*
72. *The area of the Domus Augustiana in the model of Rome. Museo della Civiltà Romana, Rome.*

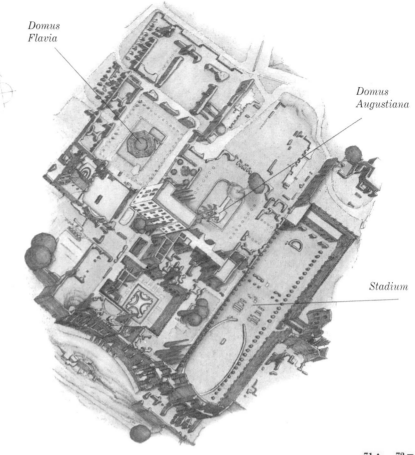

Domus Flavia

Domus Augustiana

Stadium

71 ▲   72 ▼

35

THE PALATINE

The Stadium

Domitian's private residence was connected with an enormous garden in the form of a stadium for chariot races, 160 metres long. Decorated by fountains, its perimeter was bounded by a two-storey portico. A spine ran down the centre of the stadium and formed the longitudinal axis around which the chariots raced. At one end an imposing stand enabled the emperor to watch the races in the Circus Maximus (p. 40) from his own palace. A little more than a century after construction of the Domus Augustiana (p. 34), the Emperor Septimius Severus ordered his baths to be built next to the Stadium as part of a vast program of architectural improvement of the slopes of the Palatine. They were set above massive vaults and their facade formed a monumental fountain called the *Septizodium*. The great arches of the baths are still clearly visible from the valley of the Circus Maximus.

73 ▲

73. *Conjectural reconstruction of the Palatine Stadium, watercolour by J.L. Pascal (1837–1920). Ecole des Beaux-Arts, Paris.*
74. *The baths of Septimius Severus.*
75. *Aphrodite, from the reign of Pius Antoninus, from the Palatine Stadium. Museo Palatino, Rome.*
76. *Plan of the Palatine Stadium, drawing by J.L. Pascal. Ecole des Beaux-Arts, Paris.*
77. *The Palatine Stadium.*

74 ▼   75 ▶

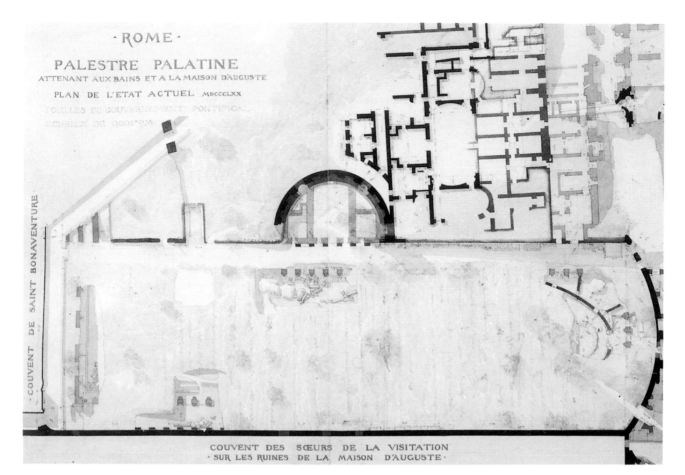

·ROME·

PALESTRE PALATINE
ATTENANT AUX BAINS ET A LA MAISON D'AUGUSTE

PLAN DE L'ETAT ACTUEL MDCCCLXX

FOUILLES DU GOUVERNEMENT PONTIFICAL

·COUVENT DE SAINT BONAVENTURE·

COUVENT DES SŒURS DE LA VISITATION
·SUR LES RUINES DE LA MAISON D'AUGUSTE·

76 ▲   77 ▼

THE MUSEO PALATINO

The earliest antiquarian museum
of the Palatine was opened in the
Domus Tiberiana (p. 30) in the later
nineteenth century. On display were
items discovered in excavations
organised by the French Emperor
Napoleon III. Then in 1882 the
government ordered that "all the
objects contained in the Museo
Palatino should be moved as soon as
possible to Santa Maria degli Angeli
alle Terme." Since then all the most
important items found on the
Palatine have been added to the
collections of the Museo delle
Terme. At the beginning of the
twentieth century there was already
a widely felt need for an
independent museum on the
Palatine; yet despite the objections
of some scholars, all finds of artistic
interest continued to be sent to the
Museo delle Terme and the
Antiquario del Palatino was used
for less valuable exhibits closely
connected with the site
and the palace.
The Museo Palatino occupies
a former convent built on top
of Domitian's Palace. Its present
display is part of a broad plan
for reorganising the various
branches of the Museo Nazionale
Romano (p. 128). Apart from
a section dedicated to Rome in the
archaic period, the museum has
displays of art in the imperial
palaces from Augustus
to late imperial times.

78. *This elegantly coiffured young
woman has been identified as one of the
daughters of the Emperor Marcus
Aurelius and his wife Faustina.*
79. *This antique-black marble herm
(a bust set on a pillar) from the
Augustan age may represent one of the
fifty Danaides that decorated the Temple
of Apollo on the Palatine.*
80. *Marble head of Apollo from
excavations of the Domus Augustiana,
dating to between the late Flavian period
and the mid-second century AD.*
81. *Also probably from the Temple
of Apollo is the fresco of Apollo
crowned with a laurel wreath
from the Augustan period.*
82. *Reconstruction of a hut erected on
the Palatine in the eighth century BC.*
83. *An ephebus carved in basalt
of the Augustan period found
near the Temple of Apollo.*

78 ▼   79 ▶

◀ 80   81 ▲

83 ▶

82 ▼

THE CIRCUS MAXIMUS

Erected in the valley between the Palatine and Aventine hills, the Circus Maximus was 600 metres long and up to 200 wide, with a spine that must have measured 340 metres. This makes it the biggest building for public spectacles of all time. The earliest installations were the work of Tarquin Priscus (seventh–sixth centuries BC), but construction proper only began in 329 BC, with the erection of the starting gates for the chariots and of the central spine. In 174 BC the seven "eggs" were placed on the spine to mark to number of circuits of the course. In 33 BC Agrippa added seven bronze dolphins. Augustus's principal addition was the obelisk of the Pharoah Ramses II (thirteenth century BC), brought from Heliopolis and erected on the spine. Much later, in 357 AD, Constantius II added a second obelisk, that of Thothmes III (fifteenth century BC) from Thebes. In 1587 both of the shattered obelisks were unearthed by Pope Sixtus V. The first was later placed in Piazza del Popolo and the second in Piazza di San Giovanni in Laterano.

The circus remained in use throughout late antiquity. The last races were held there in 549 AD by Totila, king of the Ostrogoths.

84 and 86. *The Circus Maximus.*
85. *Two-horse chariot in the circus, inlaid coloured marbles, gemstones, glass paste and mother-of-pearl of the fourth century AD, from the Basilica of Junius Bassus on the Esquiline. Museo Nazionale Romano Palazzo Massimo, Rome.*
87. *The Circus Maximus in the model of Rome. Museo della Civiltà Romana, Rome.*

40

86 ▲   87 ▼

RACES AT THE CIRCUS

The race-track in the circus was divided down the middle by a masonry spine with a pillar (*meta*) at each end to mark the turns. The chariots, drawn by two or four horses, were extremely light and it took great skill on the part of the charioteers to keep them from overturning (though disastrous falls were one of the attractions for spectators). The skill of the charioteer lay in taking the turns as close as possible so as to gain ground. The rules allowed all sorts of foul play to obstruct opponents and send them crashing into the walls. Horses and chariots were divided into teams, distinguished by different colours, and each had its supporters: the various colours eventually formed factions and had a notable influence on political life. The charioteers were idolised and if particularly skilful would accumulate immense fortunes. One Diocles, of Portuguese origin, raced for the Reds for twenty-four years in the second century AD: he won 3000 times with a two-horse chariot and 1462 times with a four-horse team. When he retired he had accumulated the fabulous sum of 35 million sesterces.

Around the circuses, like football stadiums today, there stood myriads of taverns, kiosks, and booths, and while the spectators on the terraces watched up to a hundred races a day, thieves, prostitutes, peddlers and hucksters of all sorts mixed with the crowd.

88. *Races in the circus, carving. Musei Vaticani, Rome.*
89. *The Circus Flaminius in a sixteenth-century reconstruction. Biblioteca Marciana, Venice.*
90. *The Circus Maximus (seventeenth century). Private collection.*
91. *Chariot race in the Circus Maximus, carving. Museo Archeologico, Foligno.*
92–95. *Charioteers with colours of the four factions in mosaics of the third century AD. From the floor of a villa at Baccano. Museo Nazionale Romano, Palazzo Massimo alle Terme, Rome.*

88 ▲   89 ▼

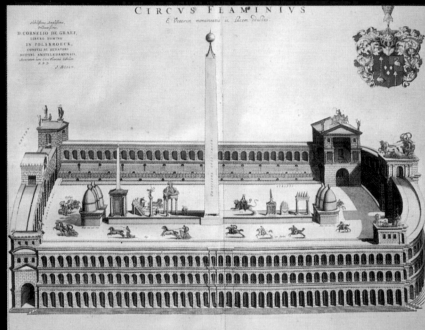

CIRCVS FLAMINIVS

90 ▼

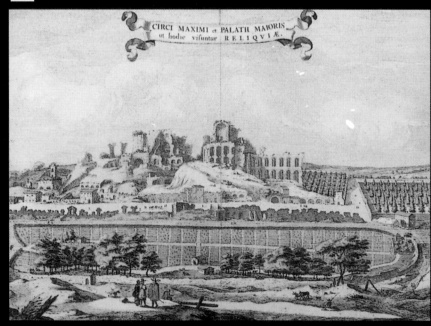

CIRCI MAXIMI et PALATII MAIORIS ut hodie visuntur RELIQVIÆ.

91 ▲

92 ▲   93 ▼

94 ▲   95 ▼

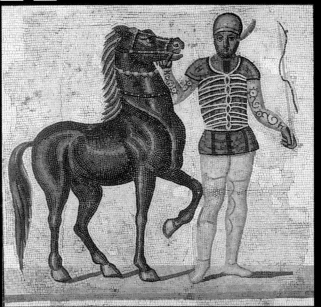

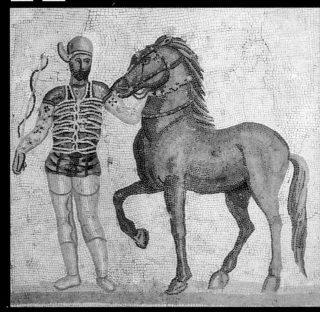

The Roman Forum

The depression occupied by the Forum, between the Palatine and the Capitol, was originally a marshy area watered by the Velabrum, a stream that flowed into the Tiber and made the whole area unhealthy. In about the seventh century BC the Velabrum was channelled into the Cloaca Maxima, a canal that drained the north-east part of Rome. The Roman Forum soon became the centre of civic life. The area was progressively occupied by religious, political and commercial buildings and then commemorative monuments. The original dirt surface was eventually paved and this was renewed several times over the centuries. The existing pavement was laid in 9 BC by order of the praetor L. Naevius Surdinus after a series of fires had destroyed much of the Forum.

For over a thousand years the Forum remained the focus of civic life and new buildings continued to be erected. Then, in the Middle Ages, it was completely forgotten and reduced to a meadow called the Campo Vaccino ("cow pasture"). The most disastrous period of its existence was the Renaissance. Pope Julius II (1503–1513), planning to rebuild Rome, pillaged the area for building materials and ancient marbles were often ground up for the lime-kiln. According to eye-witnesses like Pirro Ligorio the destruction of ancient monuments went on rapidly: at times a whole building, almost perfectly preserved, would be demolished in a month, despite the protests of Raphael or the misgivings of Michelangelo. When the spoliation was complete the area reverted to cow pasture until the last century, when the Forum was carefully explored by the first archaeologists of modern times.

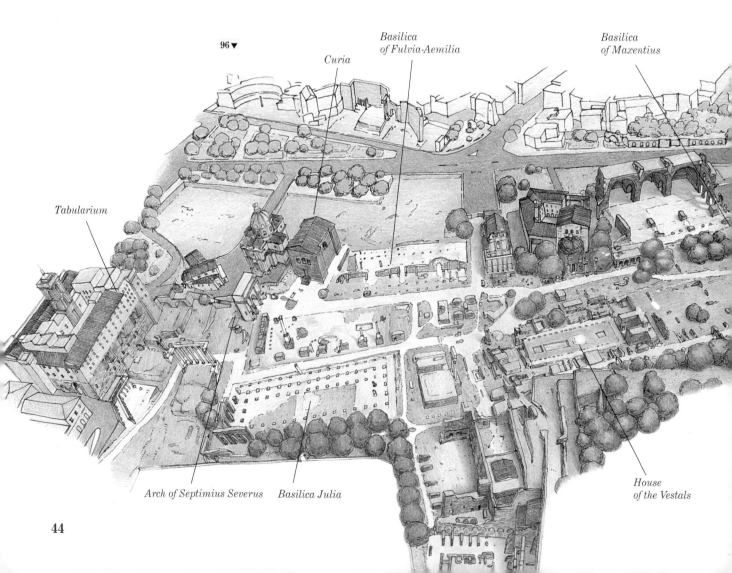

96 ▼

Curia

Basilica of Fulvia-Aemilia

Basilica of Maxentius

Tabularium

Arch of Septimius Severus   Basilica Julia

House of the Vestals

97 ▲   98 ▼

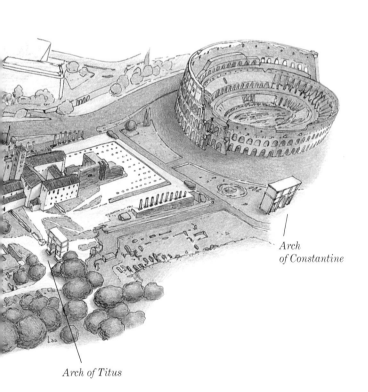

Arch
of Constantine

Arch of Titus

96. *The Forum, drawing of the present state.*
97. *View of the Forum at night.*
98. *The Forum (conjectural reconstruction and present state.)*

THE BASILICAS

Normally the legal, political, and commercial business of the forum was conducted out of doors, but in bad weather it was moved into great roofed halls called basilicas. Two rows of regular columns divided the interiors into a nave and two side aisles. The nave was built higher so that windows could be set in its sides to light the interior.

The only basilica to survive from the republican period is the Basilica Fulvia Aemilia erected in 179 BC by the censors Marcus Aemilius Lepidus and Marcus Fulvius Nobilior. Its present form is the result of extensive restoration in the imperial period.

The construction of the Basilica Julia between the two main streets from the Tiber to the Forum—the *Vicus Iugarius* and the *Vicus Tuscus*—probably entailed their deviation and the relaying of the road surface. The building, which was commissioned by Julius Caesar in 54 BC, was finished nearly fifty years later under Augustus. Its present appearance is the result of restoration under Diocletian.

THE ROMAN FORUM

103 ▲   104 ▼

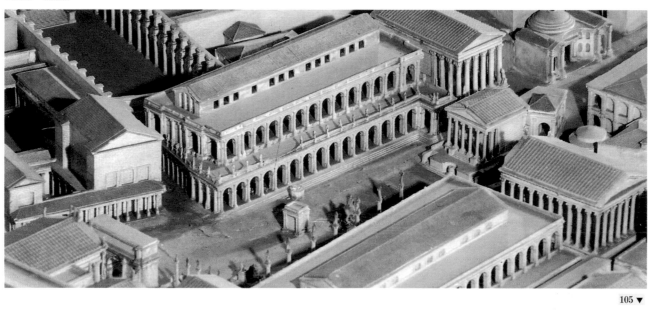

105 ▼

99. *Decoration of the Basilica Aemilia, from the period of Julius Caesar. Antiquarium del Foro, Rome.*
100. *The game of merels on the steps of the Basilica Julia.*
101–102. *Views of the Forum.*
103. *The Basilica Aemilia.*
104. *The Basilica Aemilia, Basilica Julia, and Temple of Antoninus and Faustina in a model of Rome. Museo della Civiltà Romana, Rome.*
105. *The Basilica Julia.*

THE CURIA

The Curia Hostilia, the Roman Senate's most ancient meeting-place, probably stood on the present site of the church of Santi Luca and Martina. The great brick edifice now called the Curia was the new Senate House, begun by order of Julius Caesar and completed by Augustus in 29 BC. In the seventh century it was turned into a church and this saved it from destruction. In the 1930s it was restored to the condition in which it was left after rebuilding by the Emperor Diocletian. The interior of the curia is a single large space covering an area of almost 500 square metres. The ceiling is 21 metres high. Much of the intarsia marble pavement still dates from the age of Diocletian, as do the architectural decorations on the walls. The three steps that run round the longer sides once supported the seats of the senators (numbering about three hundred), while at the far end is the dais for the president. The bronze doors are a copy of those dating from the reign of Diocletian. In the seventeenth century the originals were moved to the basilica of San Giovanni in Laterano, where they can still be seen in the central portal.

106 ▲

107 ▲

108 ▼

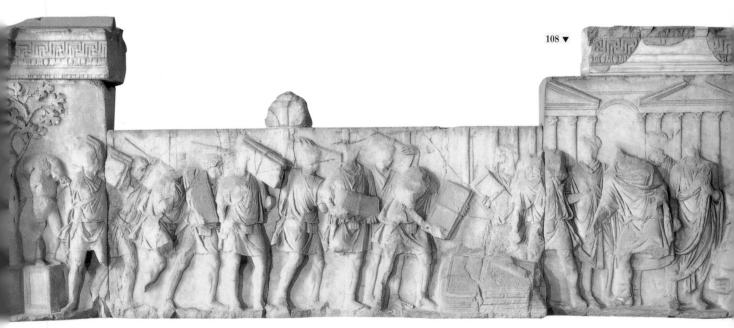

109 ▲

106–107. *The Curia Julia, view of the exterior and interior.*
108. *Marble carvings, perhaps the parapets of the tiered seating, with scenes of the reign of Trajan (98–117 AD): destruction of the debt rolls and (right) institution of the public food supply.*
109. *Cicero arraigns Catiline in the Senate. Painting by G. Maccari (1840–1919). Palazzo Madama, Rome.*

108 ▼

THE WEST SIDE

The west side of the Forum is dominated by remains of the imposing colonnades of the portico of the *Consentes di* (the counselling deities), and the temples of Vespasian, Titus, and Saturn. The original plan of the Temple of Saturn dates from the fifth century BC; it survives now in a reconstruction from the third century AD. In 303 AD to commemorate the twentieth year of the rule of Diocletian and Maximinian and the tenth year of government by Galerius and Constantius Chlorus, a monument was erected of which only the base of a column now survives: originally it must have supported a statue of Constantius Chlorus. The base, known as the "base of the Decennials" is decorated by two great figures of Victory and scenes of sacrifice in which the emperor himself takes part, assisted by various deities, including Mars and the goddess Rome. In 608 the hexarch of Italy Smaragdus dedicated a celebratory monument to the Emperor Phocas: according to the inscription on the base it was a column surmounted by a golden statue. The column and its Corinthian capital are still visible not far from the Temple of Saturn. Probably taken from a building of the third century AD, it was the last monument erected in the Forum. In the travertine pavement immediately to the east of the column of Phocas can be seen the bronze inscription that commemorates the re-paving of the Forum under Augustus by command of the urban praetor L. Naevius Surdinus. The inscription was restored in 1955.

110 ▲   111 ▼

110–111. *Remains of the west side of the Forum and a conjectural reconstruction of the monumental complex in a watercolour by C. Mayo (1835–1911). Ecole des Beaux-Arts, Paris.*
112. *The Temple of Saturn and, left, the Temple of Vespasian and Titus.*
113. *The Column of Phocas.*
114–115. *Details of the base of the Decennials: procession of senators and (bottom) animals led to sacrifice).*

50

112 ▲   113 ▼

114 ▲   115 ▼

THE ARCH OF SEPTIMIUS SEVERUS

In 203 AD the Senate erected a great arch to commemorate the victories of Septimius Severus against the Parthians, a people of Asia Minor. This triple-vaulted monument was erected just where the Via Sacra begins to climb toward the Capitol, the culminating point of triumphal processions awarded to victorious generals. The arch is wholly sheathed in marble and an image on a coin shows it was originally surmounted by bronze sculptures: a chariot drawn by six horses flanked with equestrian statues symbolising the triumph decreed to the emperor.

In the carvings on the arch the same theme is expressed in the small frieze above the two lesser vaults. This shows carts filled with booty, soldiers, prisoners, and the great statue of a seated figure that personifies the conquered province. On the attic is carved the dedication: in the fourth line the name of Septimius Severus's younger son Geta was effaced by order of his brother Caracalla, who had him put to death and decreed the "condemnation of his memory" (*damnatio memoriae*).

116 ▲▲   117 ▶

116. *Details of carvings on the Arch of Septimius Severus.*
117. *Septimius Severus (193–211 AD). Museo Nazionale Romano, Rome.*
118. *Arch of Septimius Severus.*

118 ▶

THE TEMPLE OF ANTONINUS AND FAUSTINA

The great temple above which the church of San Lorenzo in Miranda was built in the seventh and eighth centuries has been identified with a fair degree of certainty from the dedicatory inscription still legible on the architrave. The temple was erected in 141 AD in honour of Faustina, the wife of Antoninus Pius, deified after her death. Twenty years later, on the death of the emperor, the first line was added to the inscription, so that the temple was rededicated to both husband and wife.

The building stands on a tall plinth preceded by a flight of brick steps, rebuilt in modern times, which has incorporated the ancient core, also made of brick. Like other monuments in the Forum, the Temple of Antoninus and Faustina risked being dismantled in the sixteenth century when the marble slabs with which it was sheathed were removed. The columns, however, withstood the workmen's efforts. Still visible are the deep grooves scored in the tops of the shafts by ropes used in the attempt to topple them.

The flower beds of different shapes and sizes to the east of the temple reproduce the forms of the tombs of the archaic burial place (Bronze Age, tenth-eighth centuries BC) discovered early last century.

119. *Antoninus Pius (138–161 AD).*
Musei Capitolini, Rome .
120. *Temple of Antoninus and Faustina.*
121. *Detail of the temple of Antoninus and Faustina in a watercolour by J.F. Menager (1783–1864). Ecole des Beaux-Arts, Paris.*

119 ▲

120 ▲   121 ▼

122 ▲   123 ▼

THE BASILICA OF MAXENTIUS

Begun at the start of the fourth century on the site of the earlier *Horrea Piperataria*, warehouses for pepper and spices, the basilica was completed by Constantine and rebuilt at the end of the century. On that occasion its orientation was radically changed. The basilica covers 6500 square meters and is divided into a large nave with side aisles. The ceiling of the nave consists of three immense cross-vaults resting on eight columns 14.5 metres tall. The last surviving column was removed by Pope Paul V to Piazza Santa Maria Maggiore, where it stands today. In the west apse there was a colossal statue erected by Maxentius and after his death recarved to represent Constantine. It was an acrolith, i.e. a statue with the head, arms and legs of marble and the rest of the body of some less precious material, in this case probably gilded bronze. The statue, brought to light in 1487, is in the Musei Capitolini.

122. *Basilica of Maxentius.*
123. *Basilica of Maxentius (conjectural reconstruction and present state.*
124. *Column from the Basilica of Maxentius, now in Piazza Santa Maria Maggiore.*

◄ 124

THE ROMAN FORUM

THE TEMPLE OF VESTA AND THE HOUSE OF THE VESTALS

Vesta was the goddess of the hearth and her worship was overseen by six priestesses from the patrician families of Rome. Chosen in childhood, between the ages of six and ten, they had to serve the goddess as virgins for at least thirty years.

The priestesses enjoyed many privileges, but those that broke their vows were condemned to the cruel punishment of being buried alive, because the blood of a Vestal could never be shed.

At the end of their priesthood they were allowed to marry, though very few of them ever did as it was supposed to be ominous.

The round temple dedicated to Vesta was rebuilt in its present form in 191 AD by Julia Domna, the wife of Septimius Severus. Next to it stood the dwelling of the priestesses, laid out around a courtyard with porticoes running round the four sides and fountains and pools in the middle. Here must have stood the numerous statues of the Vestal Virgins revealed in excavations. The priestesses lived in comfortable rooms heated with stoves on the upper floor and had numerous warm baths for their use.

◀ 125   126 ▲   127 ▼

125. *Remains of the Temple of Vesta.*
126. *Atrium of the House of the Vestal Virgins.*
127. *The Temple of Vesta (in the middle) and the House of the Vestals (behind it) in a model of Rome, Museo della Civiltà Romana.*
128. *Vestal in the atrium of the House of the Vestals.*

128 ▶

SENATVS POPVLVSQVE ROMA
DIVO TITO DIVI VESPASIANI E
VESPASIANO AVGVSTO

◄ 129   130 ▲   131 ▼   132 ►

THE ROMAN FORUM

THE ARCH OF TITUS

The arch was erected by the Senate and people of Rome in memory of the Emperor Titus. The monument, not mentioned by ancient writers, can be identified by the dedicatory inscription still legible on the side toward the Colosseum.

The monument has a single archway and a small frieze running round the four sides above the architrave. It represents Vespasian and Titus's triumph over the Jews in 71 AD after the destruction of Jerusalem.

The carved panel on the south side within the arch depicts soldiers bearing away the plunder from the temple of Jerusalem: they include the silver trumpets and seven-branched candelabrum, of which this is the oldest representation.

In the Middle Ages the arch, like the Colosseum, was incorporated into the fortress of the Frangipane family and so survived. As can be seen in the inscription facing the Forum, in 1882 Pope Pius VII commissioned the architect Giuseppe Valadier to restore the pillars damaged by the creation of a little room inside the archway.

129. *Onyx cameo with the bust of Titus (79–81 AD). Museo Archeologico Nazionale, Florence.*
130. *Dedication to Titus on the arch in a watercolour by B. Bellotto (1720–1780).*

Accademia Carrara, Bergamo.
131. *Arch of Titus in a painting by A.L.R. Ducros (1748–1810). Musée Cantonal des Beaux-Arts, Lausanne.*
132. *The Arch of Titus.*

THE TEMPLE OF VENUS AND ROME

The most important temple in Rome was designed by Hadrian. Begun in 121 AD, construction was interrupted by the emperor's death and it was finally completed by his successor Antoninus Pius. Hadrian demolished the portico, all that remained of the monumental entrance to the Domus Aurea p. 18). He used twenty-four elephants to move the Colossus of Nero from its original position, altered the head and transformed it definitively into a representation of the Sun. Finally he artificially enlarged the summit of the Velia to create a platform capable of accommodating the building. The temple, surrounded by a colonnaded portico, had two cells facing in opposite directions: they housed the cult statues of Rome on the side toward the Forum) and Venus (the side toward the Colosseum).

Hadrian's plan, based on Greek models, brought him into conflict with Trajan's architect, Apollodorus of Damascus, who outspokenly criticised the lack of a tall plinth to support the building and the disproportion between the statue and the cell. Cassius Dio reports that he commented, "'If the gods wanted to stand up and walk out they could not.' This sharp written reply angered and troubled Hadrian who felt he had committed an irremediable error." Apollodorus was put to death for his outspokenness.

133 ▲   134 ▼

133. *Temple of Venus and Rome (conjectural reconstruction and present state).*
134. *Hadrian (117–134 AD). Museo Nazionale Romano, Rome.*
135. *Temple of Venus and Rome.*
136. *Conjectural reconstruction of the Temple of Venus and Rome (with the Colossus of Nero in the foreground) in a watercolour by E.G. Coquart (1831–1903). Ecole des Beaux-Arts, Paris.*

The Imperial Forums

When the republic came to an end the Roman Forum seemed inadequate for the functions of administration and display required of a city that was the capital of an empire extending from Gaul—modern France—to Syria. Consequently Julius Caesar began construction of a new monumental complex, which at first appeared merely the extension of the original Forum, though it also made some radical changes.

In the course of the next hundred and fifty years and the reigns of many emperors a new architectural complex grew up round the Imperial Forums to house the centre of government. The new development covered about nine hectares of land, mostly privately owned and already covered with buildings which had to be purchased and demolished. Clearly the cost of the operation, though phased over a long period, must have been astronomic.

The Imperial Forums, for centuries the centre of the city's life, were the preferred spot for displaying statues and inscriptions to the great men and women of Rome and victorious generals. Its principal function, however, was to provide adequate space for the public and religious ceremonies by which the Roman state displayed itself in all its majesty to its citizens and subjects.

137 ▼   138 ▶

137–138. *Two views of the Imperial Forums.*

THE JULIAN FORUM

In 54 BC Cicero purchased on Caesar's behalf a piece of land where a new forum was built. It was 160 metres long and 75 wide, surrounded on three sides by a double colonnade and closed on the west side by the Temple of Venus Genetrix. In the middle of the square stood an equestrian statue of Caesar (actually an existing statue of Alexander with the head recarved).

Construction of the forum was a lengthy process and was only completed after Caesar's death. In 46 BC Octavian inaugurated the temple dedicated to Venus, the mythical founder of the Gens Iulia, or Julian clan, in fulfillment of a vow by Caesar before the decisive battle against Pompey at Pharsalia (48 BC).

139. *Julius Caesar. Musei Vaticani, Rome.*
140. *The Julian Forum, conjectural reconstruction and present state.*
141. *Architectural details.*

◄ 139   140 ▲   141 ▼

THE FORUM OF NERVA

142. *The Forum of Nerva.*
143. *Remains of the Forum of Nerva in a drawing by G.P. Piranesi (1720–1728).*
144. *Nerva (96–98 AD). Palazzo Massimo alle Terme, Rome.*

142 ▲   143 ▼   144 ►

Construction of the Forum of Nerva was decided by Domitian to give monumental form to the vacant strip of land at the point where the two existing forums met. The emperor died shortly before the work was completed and it was finished by Nerva, at the time aged sixty-six, who gave it his name.

The new forum, 120 metres long and 45 wide, allowed no space for the construction of a new colonnade, so the portico of the Temple of Peace was used. At one end a temple was dedicated to Minerva: this stood till 1606 when Pope Paul V had it pulled down to provide materials for the construction of the Acqua Paola on the Janiculum.

THE FORUM OF AUGUSTUS

The construction of the Forum of Augustus, with surface area of over a hectare, was decided by a vow pronounced by Octavian, later the Emperor Augustus, before the battle of Philippi against Caesar's assassins (42 BC). Its significance lies in the temple to Mars Ultor (the Avenger) that dominates its north side.

Work on the new forum went on for almost forty and it was inaugurated in 2 BC. The function of this monumental space was to provide greater space for the crowd than the Roman Forum (p. 44) and Caesar's Forum (p. 64). But it became above all a centre of display designed to glorify the emperor, who is represented on a majestic triumphal chariot in the middle of the square.

The Forum of Augustus had a distinctively military character: it was here that the senate would meet to declare war or peace and here were erected the statues of victorious generals, who were no longer awarded a triumph as this was now the exclusive privilege of the emperors.

145 ▲   146 ▼

147 ▶

148 ▲   149 ▼

145. *Forum of Augustus, model.*
146. *Forum of Augustus.*
147. *Augustus, copy of a bronze original (20 BC) commissioned by Livia after his death for her villa at Prima Porta. Rome, Musei Vaticani.*
148–149. *Architectural details of the forum of Augustus.*

67

THE FORUM OF TRAJAN

This forum was built by the Emperor Trajan between 107 and 113 AD. It was financed by the immense wealth from the conquest of Dacia (modern Romania). Work was supervised by the most famous architect of the day, Apollodorus of Damascus. Since the space between the existing forum and the hillsides was already taken up by buildings, Apollodorus had to cut into the ridge between the Quirinal and the Capitol. The new complex was truly immense (300 × 85 metres). The forum proper was entered through a monumental arch with a single vault. The two longer sides were colonnaded and in the middle stood an imposing equestrian statue of Trajan.

The extensive clearances of the 1930s brought to light only part of the forum: most of the area is still concealed under the modern roadway and gardens. Against the background of the forum rise the remains of the Basilica Ulpia, which contained important state archives and two libraries designed by Apollodorus, one utilized to store records in Latin and the other for those in Greek, a reflection of the empire's bilingualism. The books, both rolls or bound codices, were kept in wooden presses set in the recesses still visible in the walls. The books were carefully catalogued and cared for by librarians, whose tasks included protecting them from damp.

150 ▼   151 ▲   152 ▼

150. *Trajan (98–117 AD), Archaeological Museum, Ankara.*
151 and 154. *The Markets of Trajan.*
152. *The Basilica Ulpia.*
153. *The forum of Trajan in the model of Rome. Museo della Civiltà Romana, Rome.*

68

THE MARKETS OF TRAJAN

The terraces cut out of the Quirinal hillsides to accommodate the Forum of Trajan were shored up by a complex of brick buildings called the Markets of Trajan. Their facade was a great exedra with a semi-circular chamber at either end, perhaps used as schoolrooms or lecture theatres. There is reliable evidence that at least in late imperial times the forum was used for courses of higher studies with access to the two libraries nearby.

The middle of the complex housed shops (*tabernae*): eleven on the ground floor and ten on the first floor, facing onto a passageway. The shops on the second floor, however, faced in the opposite direction and opened onto a street running behind the Markets, the Via Biberatica. The name, recorded only in the Middle Ages, was derived from the Latin noun *biber* (drink) and probably indicates that some of the shops were taverns and sold refreshments.

The Markets of Trajan were also occupied by retailers, but their principal use must have been as wholesale warehouses dealing in provisions and run by the state. They thus formed the last link in a chain of distribution that also included Trajan's important new port at Fiumicino.

155 ▲   156 ▶

155. *Head of a woman, found in the area of the Markets of Trajan.*
156–157. *Markets of Trajan.*
158. *Sign of a shop selling vegetables and poultry. From the later second century AD. Museo Archeologico, Ostia.*

157 ▲ 158 ▼

TRAJAN'S COLUMN

159 ▲   160 ▼   161 ▶

The column erected by Trajan between the two libraries in his forum is made up of nineteen cylindrical blocks of marble. Set on a pedestal and topped by a great capital, the column measures 29.78 metres or one hundred Roman feet: a carefully calculated height. The shaft of the column once supported a statue of Trajan that disappeared in the Middle Ages and was replaced by one of St. Peter in the sixteenth century. It rests on a cube-shaped plinth decorated with trophies and shields carved in very low relief. A door is set in the base with an inscription above it stating that the primary purpose of the monument was to indicate the original height of the hill excavated to construct the Forum of Trajan (p. 68).

On the emperor's death his ashes were placed on a marble ledge inside a chamber that occupied the whole north side of the base. This confirms that the column was designed and built as Trajan's funerary monument.

159. *Trajan's Column in the Napoleonic period. Anonymous watercolor of the nineteenth century. Biblioteca dell'Istituto di Storia dell'Arte, Rome.*
160. *Modern copy of a statue of Trajan. Fori Imperiali, Rome.*
161. *Detail of carvings on Trajan's Column.*
162. *Trajan's column.*

162 ▶

CARVINGS ON THE COLUMN

The decoration of Trajan's column is without precedent. It is a continuous carved frieze about 200 metres long, originally painted, which unfolds i██████l around the shaft of the column. It illustrates episodes of the two wars waged and won by Trajan against the Dacians in 101–102 and 105–106 AD. The scenes from the two campaigns are separated by the figure of Victory writing on a shield. The artist's intention was to provide a faithful record of events as they actually occurred. Given the column's placing between the two libraries and the form of the carvings, it is likely that it was a reproduction of an ancient book in roll form and the carvings were a figurative representation of Trajan's *Commentaries*, now lost, written in Dacia. The frieze depicts minutely the main episodes of the war, though they repeat the same sequence of incidents: from the beginning of the ██████ enterprise with the crossing of the Danube on a bridge of boats to the deportation of the vanquished population, with battles, sieges, the construction of camps, speeches to the troops, and executions. The figure of Trajan appears no fewer than sixty times.

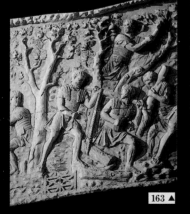

164 ▲

166 ▲

168 ▲

163 ▲

163. *Detail of the carvings.*
164–169. *Anonymous (sixteenth century), drawings of the reliefs on Trajan's Column, details. Two embassies of Dacians before Trajan (164); Trajan with a group of women prisoners (165); Dacian cavalry drowned while crossing a stream (166); the Dacians flee into a forest pursued by Numidian cavalry (167); sacrifice in camp (168); sacrifice before the great bridge on the Danube (169). Private collection.*

165 ▲

167 ▲

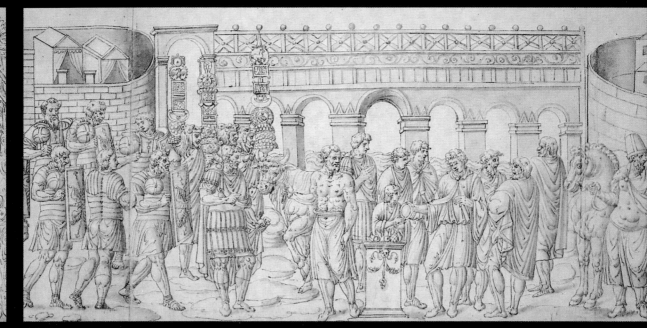

169 ▲

75

The Campus Martius

The Campus Martius or Field of Mars was an area of floodplain lying in the great bend of the Tiber and stretching to the slopes of the Pincius, Capitol and Quirinal. It was originally a pasture outside the city's religious boundary (called the *pomerium*) within which it was forbidden to bear arms. For this reason it was free of buildings—though they gradually encroached—and used for military reviews and exercises. The middle of the Campus Martius was occupied by the *Saepta*, a large rectangular space covering over 10,000 square metres. Here the *comitia tributa*, assemblies of the common people, were held.

The construction of monumental urban architecture on the Campus Martius began under the republic, in the second century BC, and culminated in a grand project conceived by Julius Caesar. He erected numerous buildings and the future Theatre of Marcellus (p. 78) and also planned to deviate the course of the Tiber to unite the Campus Martius with the Vatican hill. Caesar's death prevented execution of the plan. In the reign of Augustus the layout of the area was further altered, largely under the influence of Agrippa. A new and intense phase of construction began after the fire of 80 AD that devastated the whole of the Campus Martius. In the second century AD the central part of the plain was used mainly for funerals of the emperors and their apotheosis (the deification of the dead ruler by his successor or the Senate), as is shown, for example, by the Column of Antoninus (p. 90).

The Campus Martius was traversed by the Via Flaminia, called the Via Lata within the city walls (the Via del Corso now follows the same route). It continued to be inhabited throughout the Middle Ages and still preserves its ancient street layout and principal blocks of buildings.

170 ▼   171 ▶

170. *Theatre of Marcellus, the side facing the Forum Holitorium.*
171. *Imaginary reconstruction of the Campus Martius in a drawing by G.B. Piranesi (1720–1778).*

IL CAMPO
MARZIO
DELL'ANTICA ROMA
OPERA
DI · G · B · PIRANESI
SOCIO DELLA · REAL · SOCIETÀ
DEGLI ANTIQVARI DI LONDRA

172. *The Theatre of Marcellus in a drawing by G.B. Piranesi (1720–1778).*
173. *East side of the Theatre of Marcellus.*
174. *The Theatre of Marcellus in the model of Rome. Museo della Civiltà Romana, Rome.*
175. *The Death of Caesar in a painting by V. Camuccini (1771–1844). Museo di Capodimonte, Naples.*
176. *Building that repeats the structure of the Theatre of Pompey Via di Grotta Pinta.*

172 ▲   173 ▼

THE THEATRE OF MARCELLUS

The new theatre was erected on a site before the Temple of Apollo Sosianus (p. 80), probably the same spot where, in the republican period, there used to be a temporary theatre. Its construction was begun by Caesar but he probably had time to do little more than clear the site by demolishing part of the Circus Flaminius. The theatre was completed by Augustus, who in 13 or 11 BC dedicated it to his nephew Marcellus, his designated heir who had died prematurely ten years earlier. The theatre was over 32 metres high and its cavea (the hemicycle, with tiers of seating for the audience) had a diameter of 130 metres and held over 15,000 people.

During the Middle Ages the building was occupied by the Savelli family and in the eighteenth century by the Orsini. The upper part of the cavea, preserved to a height of 20 metres, is now incorporated into a palace designed at the start of the sixteenth century by Baldassarre Peruzzi. Its present appearance and isolation from the buildings round it are the result of demolition work in 1926–1932.

174 ▼

THE THEATRE AND CURIA OF POMPEY

Construction of the complex began in 61 BC, after Pompey's triple triumph (p. 14) and continued for five years. The porticoes, once decorated with statues, have not survived; the only remains are some relics of the great rectangular exedra which opened out in front of the theatre and was used for meetings of the senate. Here, at the foot of Pompey's statue, Caesar was assassinated on 15 March, 44 BC. Far better preserved is the theatre itself: its inner curve is repeated in the elevation of the apartment block on Via di Grotta Pinta. The inauguration of the theatre, which could hold over 17,000 people, was celebrated with sumptuous entertainments.

175 ▲   176 ▼

THE CAMPUS MARTIUS

THE TEMPLES OF APOLLO SOSIANUS AND BELLONA

Following a plague epidemic, in 431 BC a temple was dedicated to Apollo the Healer on the site of an earlier shrine to the same deity. It was repaired and refurbished on various occasions, then in 34 BC wholly rebuilt, probably by Gaius Sosius, slightly set back from its previous position. The new temple was richly decorated and had a marble floor. The pediment depicted a battle with Amazons before the goddess Athene: these carvings date from the fifth century BC and were taken from a Greek temple. The interior of the cell was like a museum, being filled with classical Greek paintings and sculpture.

East of the temple can be seen the remains of the Temple of Bellona, built by Appius Claudius Caecus after 296 BC. Sessions of the Senate were frequently held in these temples, especially when decreeing a triumph.

177 ▶
◀ 178
179 ▼

177. *The Temple of Apollo Sosianus.*
178 and 180–181. *Amazon on Horseback, Head of Nike and Theseus (circa 450–425 BC): fragments of the decoration of the pediment of the Temple of Apollo Sosianus. Centrale Montemartini, Rome.*
179. *Partial reconstruction of the Temple of Apollo Sosianus. Centrale Montemartini, Rome.*

THE PORTICO OF OCTAVIA

The north side of the Circus Flaminius, erected in 221 BC and now demolished, was bounded by a number of great porticoes. The only one to survive is the Portico of Octavia: originally erected in 146 BC by the future consul Quintus Caecilius Metellus Macedonicus, it was rebuilt in the Augustan period. During its reconstruction between 33 and 23 BC—formally attributed to Augustus's sister Octavia—the portico was enlarged to its present dimensions by incorporating the Curia and library of Octavia. Among the works of art that decorated the portico there was the statue of Cornelia, the mother of the Gracchi (the first likeness of a woman to be exhibited publicly at Rome, in around 100 BC). There were also thirty-four equestrian statues by the Greek sculptor Lysippus, taken by Metellus from the shrine of Dion in Macedonia. They portrayed Alexander the great and those of his knights who died at the battle of the Granicus.

182–183. *The Portico of Octavia.*
184. *The Portico of Octavia, drawing by G.B. Piranesi (1720–1778).*
185. *Temple B in the Sacred Precinct of Largo Argentina.*
186. *A column of temple A in the Sacred Precinct of Largo Argentina.*

◀ 182   183 ▲   184 ▼

THE SACRED PRECINCT
OF LARGO ARGENTINA

In this precinct stand four temples, of which only two were known from ancient times. The others were discovered by chance during building work in the 1920s. Fortunately their importance caused the authorities to suspend work and the monuments were preserved.

The most ancient of the buildings is known as temple C and dates from the late fourth or early third century BC. It stands on a tall tufa plinth and is decorated with terracotta ornaments. Its present appearance and the travertine paving of the whole area are due to restoration under Domitian after a fire in 80 BC.

The most recent of the three other buildings, all from republican times, is temple B. It is circular and stands on a plinth with a flight of travertine steps in front. Next to it have been found parts of a colossal acrolith of a female deity: the head and neck alone are a metre and a half tall.

THE CAMPUS MARTIUS

83

THE PANTHEON

The Pantheon was a temple originally built between 27 and 25 BC by Marcus Vipsanius Agrippa, Augustus's son-in-law, as part of his general improvement of the district. Its present appearance, however, is due to rebuilding under Hadrian. The maker's stamp in the bricks enables the rebuilding to be dated to between 118 and 125 AD. The original building was radically modified, the orientation of the facade altered, and the great rotunda added. An inscription still legible on the architrave attributes the construction to Agrippa during his third consulship. In late antiquity the Byzantine Emperor Phocas donated the monument to Pope Boniface IV, who in 609 turned it into the church of Santa Maria ad Matyres. As with other ancient buildings this conversion saved it from complete destruction, though alterations were made: the facade was raised on a flight of steps with a large rectangular porticoed square before it.

The great bronze portal, though much restored, may be the Roman original. The interior is dominated by the gigantic dome, 43.30 metres in diameter, the biggest masonry dome ever built. The perfectly harmonious appearance of the building is due to its proportions: the distance between the floor and the summit of the dome is equal to its diameter, so creating a perfect sphere inside it. The dome is decorated by five concentric tiers of coffering which narrow to a circular opening almost 9 metres across. There are numerous recesses set in the walls which once contained the statues of gods and goddesses. The Pantheon was dedicated to the twelve celestial deities and from them it took its name: the Latin word *pantheon* derives from a Greek term composed of *pân* meaning "all" and *theós* or "god."

187 ▲   188 ▼

189 ▼   190 ▶

187. *The Pantheon at night.*
188. *The Pantheon in the model of Rome. Museo della Civiltà Romana, Rome.*
189. *Detail of the interior of the Pantheon in a watercolour by G. Chedanne (1861–1940). Ecole des Beaux-Arts, Paris.*
190. *Pantheon, view of the interior.*

THE STADIUM
OF DOMITIAN

Piazza Navona is one of the most important examples of continuity between ancient and modern Rome, and a fine example of urban design. Its elongated rectangular form, with one of the shorter sides curved, exactly repeats the design of the Stadium of Domitian. This was constructed in about 86 AD for the Greek athletic competitions. Measuring 275 metres long by over 10 in width, it had two tiers of seating which held up to three thousand spectators. The two principal entrances were in the middle of the longer sides and the race track itself was left completely clear.

The rich sculptural decorations of the stadium must have included the statue of Pasquino, now on the corner of Palazzo Braschi in Piazza Pasquino. The obelisk placed at the centre of Piazza Navona in 1651 by Gian Lorenzo Bernini—on the fountain of the Rivers which he designed —came from the Circus of Maxentius on the Via Appia, though probably it was originally part of a different monument.

191. ▲

192. ▲   193. ▼

191. *The stadium of Domitian on a coin minted by Septimius Severus in 202–203 AD to commemorate the return of the emperor and his son Caracalla as well as the latter's marriage to Plautilla. Games to celebrate the marriage were held in the stadium. British Museum, London.*
192. *Remains of the Stadium of Domitian. Piazza Navona, Rome.*
193. *Piazza Navona, early twentieth century.*
194–195. *Piazza Navona.*

THE TEMPLE OF HADRIAN

Construction of the Temple of Hadrian probably began in 139 AD, the year of the emperor's deification. Consecrated six years later, the building had eight columns on the shorter sides and fifteen on the longer. The cell was decorated with a series of pillars with carvings representing the provinces of the empire: the surviving examples are now in the Musei Capitolini (p. 130). Eleven columns are still visible on the right side of the temple: their preservation is due to the reuse of the temple in the course of the centuries. Sixteenth-century drawings already show the columns incorporated into a sort of castle with numerous small windows. The fundamental transformation dates from 1695, when the architect Francesco Fontana designed the Dogana di Terra (Customs House): he incorporated the surviving temple structures in the harmonious facade of his three-storey building, set with large windows. It is now the premises of the Rome Stock Exchange. Clearly visible inside are the remains of the cell of the temple with its coffered barrel-vaulting.

◄ 196   197 ▲

196. *Coin of Innocent XII with the Dogana di Terra.*
197. *The Temple of Hadrian in a photo of 1868.*
198. *Personifications of the Roman provinces and a trophy on a carving from the Temple of Hadrian (145 AD). Musei Capitolini, Rome.*

198 ▼

THE COLUMN OF MARCUS AURELIUS

Erected between 180 (the date of the emperor's death) and 196 AD, this column records the feats of Marcus Aurelius against the Germans and Sarmatians. An inscription states that in the latter year a certain Adrastus, the caretaker of the column, was authorised to re-use the wooden scaffolding to build himself a house.

The monument is modelled on Trajan's column (p. 72). Nineteen circular blocks of stones set one above the other stand 100 Roman feet high (just under 30 metres). The tall base, decorated by a frieze with figures of Victory and a scene of submission by barbarians, was demolished in 1589 by Pope Sixtus V, who also replaced the emperor's statue at the top with the figure of St. Paul.

The record of the deeds of Marcus Aurelius forms a continuous narrative spiralling round the shaft. The first carving shows the Roman army crossing the Danube by a bridge; this is followed by various dramatic episodes alternating with genre scenes. As on Trajan's column the figure of Victory divides the narrative into two parts, which probably depict the campaigns of 172–173 and 174–175 AD.

◀ 199   200 ▲ ▲   201 ▶

199. *The Column of Marcus Aurelius in a drawing by G.B. Piranesi (1720–1778).*
200. *Two details of the carvings on the column.*
201. *Marcus Aurelius (161–180 AD). Rome, Musei Capitolini.*

THE COLUMN OF ANTONINUS PIUS

When Antoninus Pius died, his adopted sons and successors Marcus Aurelius and Lucius Verus erected a monument to his honour in the Campus Martius, close by the place where the emperor's body was cremated. The marble base, decorated with carvings (now in the Vatican Museums), was surmounted by a red granite column designed by the architect Heraclides. The shaft of the column has been lost, except for the summit, which bore an inscription, the architect's signature and the date the stone was quarried. The rest was carved up and used to restore the nearby sundial of Augustus.

The principal relief on the base depicts the apotheosis of the emperor and his wife Faustina, borne to the sky by the winged genius Aion, the symbol of eternity. The two sides are decorated with almost identical scenes: a ring of cavalry encircling a parade of infantry, in allusion to the consecration of the imperial couple on the site of the funeral pyre.

202. *Antoninus Pius (138–161 AD). Museum of Sculpture, Munich.*
203. *Apotheosis of Antoninus and Faustina, base of the Column of Antoninius Pius. Musei Vaticani, Rome.*

202 ▼   203 ►

◄ 204   205 ▲   206 ►

THE ARA PACIS

THE CAMPUS MARTIUS

The decision in 14 BC to build the Ara Pacis, the great altar of peace, and its consecration by Augustus five years later, is recounted by the emperor himself in his chronicle of his achievements. During the reign of Hadrian, the marked rise in the height of the terrain around it made it necessary to isolate the monument, of which only the frieze at the top remained visible.

The monument, wholly of marble, is a rectangular enclosure with two great doors on the longer sides. It is set on a podium with access provided by a flight of steps. Inside this the altar proper stands on three steps which run all the way round it; another five steps allowed the priest to reach the horizontal plane of the altar.

The rediscovery of the first fragments of the Ara Pacis date from 1568, when nine blocks of carved stone were found in the foundations of Palazzo Almagìa. At various times in the nineteenth century further carvings were found and identified as part of the altar. In 1937–1938, to celebrate the second millennium of the emperor's birth, the Ara Pacis was re-assembled not far from its original site.

204–205. Details of the reliefs on the Ara Pacis: Procession of the Quirites and (on the right) procession of the Julio-Claudian family.
206. Antonia Augusta as Venus Genetrix, commissioned by her son Claudius in 45 AD for the nymphaeum of the palace at Baia. Baia Bacoli, Castello Aragonese, Naples.
207. The Ara Pacis.

207 ▼

THE RELIEFS ON THE ARA PACIS

The Ara Pacis epitomised Augustus's policy and ideology, as well as the art of the age. The processional frieze was the work of Greek artists inspired by the carvings on the Parthenon, the most celebrated monument of classical Greece. The lower part of the outside wall of the Ara Pacis is decorated with a frieze of vegetable motifs. The upper part, flanking the entrance, has allegorical images that reflect the legend of the founding of Rome. Reliefs at the sides depict the official procession held for consecration of the altar: it opens with the lictors bearing the fasces, the of authority, before the magistrate. They are followed by the priests, including Augustus as Pontifex Maximus, and the imperial family, faithfully portrayed: we can identify Augustus's wife Livia with his sons Tiberius, the future emperor, and Drusus. The procession depicted on the Ara Pacis was not so much the record of an actual event as the official representation of a dynasty: the procession never took place as depicted, since in 14 BC, when it was decided to build the altar, Augustus was not yet Pontifex Maximus, and when the monument was consecrated in 9 BC his son-in-law Agrippa, depicted in the relief, had already died.

208. *The Ara Pacis, reconstruction.*
209–212. *Detail of the carvings on the Ara Pacis: the infant Gaius Caesar (209); Peace (210); Domitian and Domitia, the children of Antonia (211); Aeneas sacrificing to the Penates (212).*

208 ▼   209 ▲

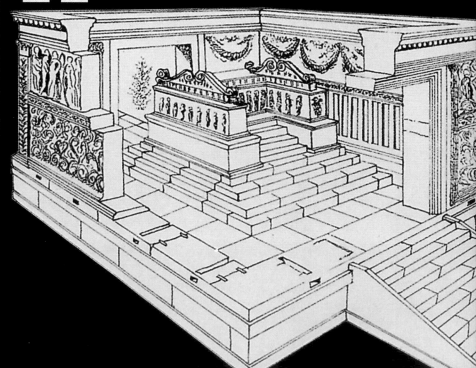

94

210 ▲

211 ▲ 212 ▼

THE MAUSOLEUM OF AUGUSTUS

In 29 BC, after conquering Egypt and visiting Alexander the Great's tomb in Alexandria, Augustus began construction of his own mausoleum as a great dynastic sepulchre for himself and his descendants. The edifice is circular and measures about 87 metres across. The door is flanked by two pillars, to which were fixed the bronze tables with Augustus's autobiography, and two obelisks, perhaps commissioned by the emperor himself: one is now stands between the statues of the Dioscuri before the Quirinal, the other by the apse of Santa Maria Maggiore. Throughout the first century AD the mausoleum was used as a tomb for the imperial family. In the Middle Ages it was converted to various uses and in quite modern times it was used for public amusements. Excavations in the 1930s cleared away all the later additions to reveal the original structure.

213 ▲ 214 ▼

213. *Mausoleum of Augustus, reconstruction.*
214. *Detail of the Mausoleum of Augustus in a drawing by G.B. Piranesi (1720–1778).*
215. *The Mausoleum of Augustus today.*
216. *Bull-fight in the Mausoleum of Augustus in a watercolour by B. Pinelli (1781–1835).*

The Fora Boarium and Holitorium

The plain between the Tiber and the Palatine, Aventine and Capitoline hills was very important early in the city's history and perhaps in even more primitive times. On this strip of territory there intersected two of the principal lines of communication of central Italy: the Tiber, navigable as far as Orte, and a road that linked Campania with Etruria, crossing the Tiber at the Insula Tiberina by the Sublician bridge (p. 114), the first to span the river. The same area was also traversed by the Via Salaria, used by the pastoral population of the Sabine hills to bring salt from the river mouth.

In archaic times the plain grew into an important trading centre, above all for goods arriving by water, with thriving cattle and vegetable markets, the Forum Boarium and Forum Holitorium.

The first conspicuous buildings were erected by a king of Etruscan origins, Servius Tullius (sixth century BC), but the most important phase of construction came in the second century BC after the area was ravaged by fire. It was then that the first warehouse was built (the *Horrea Aemiliana*), probably by Scipio Aemilianus, replaced in the imperial period by a complex of brick buildings.

The Arch of the Argentarii, perhaps originally an entrance to the Forum Boarium, stands near the church of San Giorgio al Velabro. The monument was dedicated by the bankers and cattle dealers to Septimius Severus and his family in 204 AD. The Arch of the Argentarii, like that of Septimius Severus, bears traces of the obliterated figures of Geta and, probably, Caracalla's wife Plautilla and her father, all assassinated by the emperor. Before the church of San Giorgio stands a great four-sided arch erected by Constans II in 357 AD when he visited Rome. The arch is cross-vaulted and the keystones of the four arches are decorated with the figures of Rome and Juno (both seated), Minerva and perhaps Ceres (standing). The attic, well preserved till 1830, was demolished in the belief it was mediaeval work.

217 ▼   218 ▶

217. *The Arch of Janus.*
218. *The Temple of Fortunus.*

THE SACRED PRECINCT OF S. OMBONO

At the foot of the Capitol lies a sacred precinct that includes two small temples dedicated to Fortune and the Mater Matuta, traditionally attributed to the period of Servius Tullius. Archaeological studies have confirmed the accounts of ancient writers by revealing a more ancient level from the later seventh or early sixth century BC, in which the only sign of cult use is an altar. The presence of an Etruscan inscription and a small ivory votive offering bearing the name of a member of the Spurinna family, originally of Tarquinia, is important evidence of the Etruscan presence in Rome and probably confirms indirectly the tradition of the dynasty of the Tarquins. The two temples, founded in about the mid-sixth century BC, were reconstructed a number of times in the republican period, always by personages in some way connected with the Etruscan world, such as Camillus after his conquest of Veii in 396 BC.

219 ▲   220 ▼

221 ▼

219–220. *The sacred precinct of Sant'Ombono.*
221. *Capital of a column.*

222 ▲   223 ▼

TEMPLES OF THE FORUM HOLITORIUM

The small square now bounded by the Tiber, the Theatre of Marcellus and the Capitol was once the ancient Forum Holitorium, the vegetable market where, in republican times, stood four temples dedicated to Janus, Spes (Hope), Juno Sospita and Pietas (this last was destroyed to build the Theatre of Marcellus). The imposing remains of the first three edifices stand beside the church of San Nicola in Carcere, partly built over them. The podium and colonnade of the Temple of Juno Sospita can be seen in the undercroft and in the front of the church. The northernmost temple, dedicated to Janus, is the best preserved, complete with a frieze. It is incorporated in the right side of the church of San Nicola.

222. *Architectural detail of the Temple of Juno Sospita.*
223. *The church of San Nicola in Carcere superimposed on the Temple of Juno Sospita.*

THE FORA BOARIUM AND HOLITORIUM

101

TEMPLES OF THE FORUM BOARIUM

The Forum Boarium, covering most of the plain between the Tiber and the Capitol, Palatine and Aventine, contains two exceptionally well-preserved little temples in what is now Piazza Bocca della Verità. The Temple of Fortune, actually identified as the temple of Portunus (an ancient tutelary God of Rome's first trading port, the Portus Tiberinus, on the bend in the river), was erected in the early monarchical period and rebuilt a number of times by the first century AD. The temple stands on a dry-stone plinth. The elevation is entirely made out of Anio tufa, except for the columns and capitals which are of travertine. The cornice is original and bears lion protomes. The so-called Temple of Vesta nearby is wholly made of Greek marble from Mount Pentelicus. Erected by a wealthy Roman oil merchant, it was in fact dedicated to Hercules, the patron of oil-sellers. Ancient records refer to it as the Temple of Hercules Victor. It stands on a stepped stone base, with a ring of twenty Corinthian columns encircling a cell with the entrance on the east side. It seems to have been the work of Hermodoros, a Greek architect from Salamis active in Rome in the later second century BC.

224. *Column of the Temple of Fortune.*
225. *The Temple of Vesta.*

224 ▼   225 ▶

The Baths

Everyone went to the baths or *thermae*: men and women, young and old, rich and poor. The rich, though they had private baths of their own, were actually assiduous visitors at the public baths, where they went accompanied by their slaves and "clients" (free men who offered their services in exchange for patronage). The clients would attend their patron at the baths, helping to perfume him with oil and invigorate him with massages. Even the emperor and members of his family went to the public baths and mingled with the crowds. Admission was cheap, in some cases free of charge, and it was possible to stay there all afternoon. The hours of opening varied through the centuries. Under the republic it was not thought necessary to bathe more than once a week but under the empire many people bathed daily. Habits, of course, varied. We know that Augustus did not care to bathe often in winter but Commodus had seven or eight complete baths every day; and Gordian I took four or five baths daily in summer and two in winter.

At the baths it was possible to follow different routines. Bathers would normally strip in the changing room and proceed to the gymnasium, where they oiled their bodies and performed exercises. From there they passed to the sweat bath (*laconicum*), and so to a hot pool (*calidarium*) and a room with small tubs filled with lukewarm water (*tepidarium*). The last stages were a large unheated chamber, often richly decorated (*frigidarium*), and the outdoor swimming pool (*natatio*).

◀ 226   227 ▶

226. *Drawing: reconstruction of a calidarium.*
227. *Seated Boxer in the Octagonal Room of the baths of Diocletian.*

THE BATHS OF DIOCLETIAN

The baths of Diocletian, the biggest ever built in Rome, were erected in one of the most densely populated parts of the city, the area comprising the Esquiline, Quirinal and Viminal. Many buildings were demolished to make way for this immense complex, built rapidly between 298 and 306 AD and covering 140,000 square metres. The central building measured 250 by 180 metres.

Some parts of the baths can still be seen, incorporated into more recent buildings. For example the church of Santa Maria degli Angeli was built in the central chamber of the baths and its entrance is set in one of the apses of the *calidarium*. The areas of the basilica which were originally part of the baths have been incorporated into the museum of the baths (Museo delle Terme). Its garden still contains the facade of the main building.

228. *Piazza Esedra and chambers of the baths of Diocletian in an aerial photo of the 1920s.*
229. *Conjectural reconstruction of the interior of the Baths of Diocletian in a watercolour by E. Paulin (1848–1915). Ecole des Beaux-Arts, Paris.*
230. *The baths of Diocletian in the model of Rome. Museo della Civiltà Romana, Rome.*

228 ▲   229 ▼

"I live on top of the public baths. Imagine a hubbub that makes you sorry you're not deaf. Whenever the athletes practise lifting lead weights ... I hear them wheezing and grunting. I even hear the masseur's hand slapping their shoulders. ... Then if the ball players arrive and start calling points aloud it's the last straw. Add ... people plunging into the swimming pool with an almighty splash and you'll have some idea of what goes on. But apart from these people, who at least have normal voices, imagine the depilator who tries to attract attention by screeching and never keeps quiet except when he's stripping the hairs from someone's armpits and making them yell instead of him. And then there's the drinks seller with his cry, and the sausage seller with his, and the other hucksters, and they all cry their wares in their own special tone of voice."
Seneca, Letters to Lucilius.

230 ▲

THE BATHS OF TITUS

The only comprehensive record we have of the baths which the Emperor Titus inaugurated in 80 AD is a plan drawn by the sixteenth-century architect Andrea Palladio. The complex was not very large and had the same orientation as Nero's Domus Aurea, which adjoined it on the east. Access was provided by a flight of steps on the side facing the Colosseum.

The extreme rapidity of its construction, mentioned by the poet Martial, and its close connection with Nero's palace next door suggest that it was simply a conversion of the sumptuous baths of the Domus Aurea. This would reflect the policy of Vespasian and his sons, who sought to restore to public use the extravagant and luxurious buildings erected by Nero for himself. Its plan is typical of all large public baths, with a central basilica and two identical suites of chambers ranged on each side of it.

◄ 231   232 ▲   233 ▼

231. *Titus (79–81 AD), from the shrine of the house of Augustus at Misenus. Castello Aragonese, Baia Bacoli, Naples.*
232. *The baths of Titus in the model of Rome. Museo della Civiltà Romana, Rome.*
233. *Stove. Museo Archeologico Nazionale, Naples.*

234 ▲   235 ▼

THE BATHS OF TRAJAN

The baths of Trajan were designed, like the emperor's other public works, by the architect Apollodorus of Damascus. He erected the new complex over the remains of the Domus Aurea, destroyed by fire in 104 AD. The baths were opened five years later.

They covered an area of over 100,000 square metres, almost half of which was occupied by the central building. Trajan's were the first large baths where the principal building was flanked by an outer court with an exedra, a model imitated in all subsequent large bathing complexes. Some remains of Trajan's Baths can be found in the park of the Oppian hill.

234. *The Baths of Trajan in the model of Rome. Museo della Civiltà Romana, Rome.*
235. *The Baths of Trajan.*

THE BATHS OF CARACALLA

The Thermae Antoninianae, the best preserved baths of the imperial period, were built by Caracalla, who dedicated the central building in 216 AD. The outer enclosure was completed by the last emperors of the house of Severus, Heliogabalus and Alexander Severus. Water was piped from a special offshoot of the Aqua Marcia known as the Aqua Antoniniana, piped to the baths across the Appian Way not far from Porta San Sebastiana.

The Baths of Caracalla could accommodate up to 1600 bathers, about half the number of the later Baths of Diocletian (p. 106). Renewed by the Emperors Aurelian and Diocletian and by Theodoric, king of the Visigoths, it ceased to function in 537, when the Goths blocked the aqueducts and cut off the water supply.

Excavations through the centuries, above all the sixteenth, revealed the rich decoration and furnishings of the complex, like the two granite baths now in Piazza Farnese.

◄ 236   237 ▲   238 ▼

236. *Caracalla (211–217). Museo Nazionale Romano (Palazzo Massimo alle Terme), Rome.*
237. *The gymnasium.*
238. *Detail of mosaic decoration (early third century AD).*
239. *The frigidarium.*
240. *The Baths of Caracalla in the model of Rome. Museo della Civiltà Romana, Rome.*

THE BATHS

The Tiber

◄ 241   242 ▲

The most ancient port of Rome was on the right bank of the Tiber, in the bend facing the Velabrum district and the Forum Boarium (p. 98). This was a cramped area which allowed no scope for expansion. After the third Punic war (late third century BC) the city's population grew rapidly, trade flourished, and it became urgent to find a site for a new port. The choice fell on the great open plain which stretched before the Aventine, and here new docks and warehouses were erected.

Behind the port, towards the Aurelian Walls, stood the *Mons Testaceus* (meaning "Hill of Potsherds"). This was a completely artificial hill, 30 metres high and about 1 kilometre around the base, created by the gradual accumulation of fragments of jars containing products that arrived by water at the port of Rome, especially between 140 BC and the third century AD. Carts would climb a ramp to the hilltop to dispose of their "empties," jars valueless once their contents were removed. The topmost layer of shards consists almost exclusively of fragments of oil jars from Spain. Often one of the handles bears the name of the producer and the side of the jar has the name of the exporter and the seals applied on departure and arrival.

243 ▼

241. *Apollo of the Tiber, copy from the age of Hadrian or the Antonines of a classical Greek original. The statue was found in the bed of the river when the embankments were being rebuilt. Museo Nazionale Romano (Palazzo Masssimo alle Terme), Rome.*
242. *The Insula Tiberina with the river in full spate in 1986.*
243. *Boat on a sea swarming with fish: fragment of a fresco from excavations at the river port of San Paolo a Lungotevere. The painting dates from 125–150 AD.*

244 ▲   245 ▼

THE ISLAND IN THE TIBER

When the plague was raging at Rome in 293 BC, the *Sibylline Books* were consulted and an embassy was sent to Epidaurus in Greece, the centre of the cult of Aesculapius, the god of medicine. Two years later a Roman trireme returned to the homeland bringing one of the sacred serpents, the symbol of the god. The snake escaped and swam from the military port on the banks of the Campus Martius to the Insula Tiberina, the island in the Tiber, where it disappeared. This was taken as an omen that a new temple to Aesculapius should be built on the island and construction began in 289 BC.

The use of the Insula Tiberina as a sanatorium, probably due to its isolation from the city, continued throughout the Middle Ages and it is still the location of the Fatebenefratelli Hospital, founded in 1548.

The islet was the object of general redevelopment in the middle of the first century BC. Bridges linking it to the mainland were built and the eastern tip was refashioned in the form of a ship's prow, so that the island itself was transformed into the image of the trireme that brought the sacred serpent, which is also represented entwined around a rod in the hand of Aesculapius.

244. *The Insula Tiberina in the model of Rome,. Museo della Civiltà Romana, Rome.*
245. *Aesculapius. Antiquarium Forense, Rome.*
246. *The Ponte Rotto and the Insula Tiberina.*
247. *The Ponte Cestio and the Insula Tiberina.*

THE TIBER

114

248 ▲   249 ▼

250 ▼

THE BRIDGES

The most ancient bridge built over the Tiber was the wooden Sublician Bridge, close to the Forum Boarium, which linked the far side of the Tiber and the Janiculum with the rest of the city. Tradition has it that the Sublician was the bridge that Horatius Cocles held against an Etruscan army under Porsenna, so allowing the Romans time to hew down its timbers and prevent the enemy entering the city.

The most ancient stone bridge was the Aemilian, built in 179 BC. Some arches of this bridge are still visible just below the Insula Tiberina. This was followed by the Milvian (or Mulvian) bridge built by Marcus Aemilius Scaurus in 109 BC, probably to replace the wooden bridge built some hundred years earlier to bring the Via Flaminia across the Tiber north of Rome. It was here that Constantine in 312 BC won his final victory over his rival Maxentius.

THE TIBER

116

251 ▲   252 ▼

253 ▶

254 ▼

248 and 251. *The Milvian Bridge*
249. *The Fabrician Bridge in the nineteenth century.*
250 and 253. *The Ponte Rotto.*
252. *The Fabrician Bridge.*
254. *The Ponte Sistino.*

THE MAUSOLEUM OF HADRIAN

The monumental tomb built by the Emperor Hadrian on the right bank of the Tiber was inspired by the Mausoleum of Augustus in the Campus Martius. To connect the mausoleum with the city Hadrian erected the Aemilian Bridge, now much altered but· still in use and called Ponte Sant'Angelo.

The mausoleum consisted originally of a base in the form of a parallelepiped, 84 metres wide and 10 high, on which rested a circular drum 64 metres across and 20 high. The whole structure was sheathed in marble and travertine and covered with a mound of earth planted with trees and ringed with statues. On the summit stood a four-horse chariot with the statue of Hadrian.

For almost a century, down to the time of Caracalla, the mausoleum was the burial place of the emperors. Transformed into a fortress in the Middle Ages it became the strong point of the Vatican's defensive system and was also used as a prison.

In the Renaissance the mausoleum took the name by which it is now known, Castel Sant-Angelo, from the statue which replaced Hadrian's on the summit of the monument.

◄ 255   256 ▲   257 ▼

118

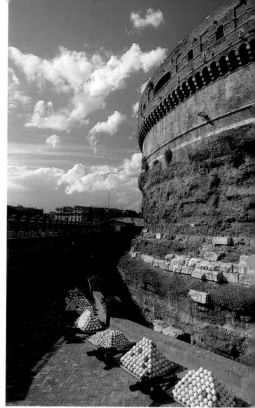

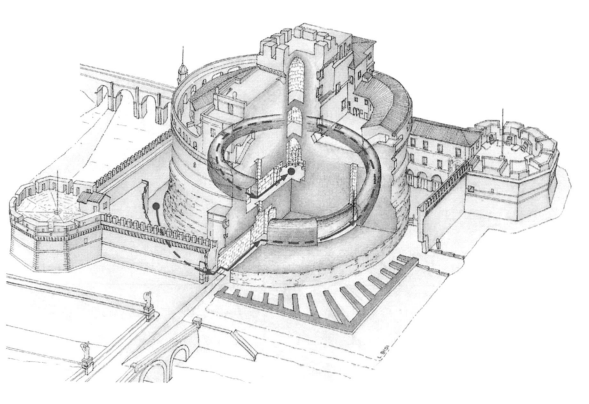

255. *Hadrian
(117–138 AD).
Israel Museum,
Jerusalem.*
256–257. *Castel
Sant'Angelo and
Ponte Sant'Angelo.*
258. *Architectural
detail of Castel
Sant'Angelo.*
259. *Castel
Sant'Angelo,
reconstruction.*

The City Walls

According to tradition, the most city's first walls were built by the sixth king of Rome, Servius Tullius (sixth century BC). The walls now visible, however, built of tufa from the quarries of Grotta Oscura, were built after the Gallic invasion. Livy says that construction of the wall was decided in 390 BC by the censors, the magistrates who oversaw public works. They used tufa from quarries that fell Rome after the conquest of Veii (396 BC). These walls enclosed an area of 426 hectares and were rebuilt on a number of occasions between the fourth century BC and 87 BC (during the civil war between Marius and Sulla).

After the republican era, however, the city remained practically without walls until 271 AD, when the Emperor Aurelian decided it was advisable to fortify Rome against Barbarian incursions, above all in the long periods when wars kept him abroad. The work went ahead rapidly and by the time of Aurelian's death in 275 most of the wall must have been built. It fell to his successor Probus to complete the work.

This wall, made of brick, was 6 metres high and 3.50 metres thick. It was fortified with square towers every hundred *passi* (equal to 29.60 metres). Its length was just under 19 kilometres and it took in numerous earlier edifices. The first emperor to strengthen it was Maxentius, but the most massive enlargement was the work of Arcadius and Honorius. Facing attacks by the Goths in 401–402 they doubled the wall's height; the path along its top patrolled by guards was replaced by a covered gallery and the Mausoleum of Hadrian was included in the fortification as a castle outpost on the right bank of the Tiber.

Other buildings were also incorporated in the Roman walls. One of the most ancient annexed during construction of Aurelian's wall was the pyramid of Caius Cestius, erected under his testament in less than 330 days. The bronze statues of Caius Cestius, now in the Musei Capitolini, were paid for with money from the sale of tapestries from Pergamum which could not be placed in the sepulchre because of a sumptuary law of 18 BC.

260. *Antonio Sangallo the Younger (1483-1546), the Bastion of Sangallo on the Aurelian Walls.*
261. *Plan of the walls.*
262. *The Servian Wall near the Stazione Termini.*
263. *The Aurelian walls and the Pyramid of Caius Cestius.*
264. *The Aurelian Walls.*

▲ 260   261 ▼   262 ▼

265 ▲   266 ▼

THE GATES

In Aurelian's project the main gates set in the walls consisted of twin entrances, covered with arches and contained within two semicircular towers. More modest entrances were simply inserted in a stretch of walls between two square towers.

In the course of the reinforcements decided by Arcadius and Honorius many of the double entrances were eliminated and the towers were raised and fortified. The gates, with an inner counter-door, were transformed into self-sufficient fortresses. The closure was doubled and consisted on the outside of a double door and on the inside of a portcullis which could be raised and lowered.

One of the best preserved stretches of the Aurelian walls between Porta Latina and Porta San Sebastiano, with the Museo delle Mura (Museum of the City Walls). Here it is also possible to walk along the top of a section of the walls.

267 ▼

270 ▲   271 ▼

268 ▲   269 ▼

272 ▼

265. *Porta San Giovanni, set in the Aurelian walls in 1574.*
266. *Porta Latina.*
267. *The Pyramid of Caius Cestius and Porta San Paolo.*
268. *Porta Pinciana: seen from the inside.*
269. *Porta Maggiore: seen from the inside.*
270. *Porta San Paolo.*
271. *Porta Maggiore: seen from the outside.*
272. *Porta San Sebastiano.*

The Aqueducts

The water supply in the great cities of the empire and Rome above all was so advanced that only modern industrialised nations have ever surpassed the Roman achievements. Rome's first aqueduct was built in the fourth century BC to bring water from Praeneste; in the imperial period a million cubic metres of water flowed daily into the city down eleven aqueducts, a quantity only surpassed by modern Rome in the 1970s.

The most celebrated Roman aqueduct was the one begun by Caligula and later completed by Claudius. The canal started from Subiaco and reached Rome after travelling over 68 kilometres. For a stretch of about 16 kilometres it was carried on magnificent tufa arches still visible in the countryside near the city gates.

An offshoot leading to the Caelius was begun by Nero, while Domitian conveyed it as far as the Palatine.

274 ▲   275 ▼

273 and 277. *The Claudian aqueduct.*
274. *Detail of Nero's aqueduct (offshoot of the Claudian aqueduct) at Porta Maggiore.*
275. *Colossal statue of Claudius as Jove (42–43 AD). Musei Vaticani, Rome.*
276. *The Colosseum and the Claudian aqueduct. Detail of a model. Museo della Civiltà Romana, Rome.*

273 ▼

The Consular Roads

The first true paved road outside Rome was the Appian Way, constructed in 312 BC by the Censor Appius Claudius Caecus to join Rome to Capua and later Brindisi. The technique for building these and other Roman roads was extremely precise and, as can still be seen, they were made to last. The first step in construction was to dig two shallow parallel trenches marking the sides of the road, which had to be at least wide enough for two carts to pass by each other. Then the roadway was dug out and foundations laid of sand and lime. This was covered for up to 1.5 metres with layers of four different materials: a bed of large stones (*statumen*), smaller stones and lime (*rudus*), sand and gravel (*nucleus*), and then a carefully laid surface of smoothed paving stones (*summum dorsum*). The roads were slightly cambered to improve runoff.

Between the third and second centuries BC other important roads were built to connect Rome with her newly conquered territories; they included the Via Cassia, Via Aurelia and Via Flaminia. The growth of the road network kept pace with the expansion of empire and the maintenance of the roads was a constant concern of all emperors.

280 ▲   281 ▼

278 ▲   279 ▶

278. *The tomb of Caecilia Metella (later first century BC).*
279. *The Villa of the Quintilii (mid-second century AD).*
280. *Title page of the* Via Appia Illustrata ab Urbe Roma ad Capuam; *illustrations by Carlo Labruzzi (eighteenth century).*
281. *Casal Rotondo, sepulchre of the Augustan period.*
282. *The Via Appia at Casal Rotondo.*

126

APPIA
STRATA
RBE·ROMA
CAPVAM

LIMITE·NOTO
M·TERITVR·REGINA·VIARVM

282 ▶

Museums

It was in the Renaissance that museums were first created to display the immense wealth of Roman remains. They were exhibited in the palaces which still house the Musei Vaticani and the Musei Capitolini. In 1734, by order of Pope Clement XII, the latter became the world's first public museum. In 1899 the Italian State instituted the Museo Nazionale Romano to create a great archaeological museum for the capital and house the immense number of relics and works of art being turned up in excavations. The Museo Nazionale Romano has recently been reorganised and is now divided between four different buildings. The collection at Palazzo Altemps (p. 138) is dedicated to antiquarian collections. Palazzo Massimo alle Terme (p. 134–137) has displays of frescoes, sculptures, mosaics and other items from late republican to late imperial times, as well as a large selection of coins and jewellery. In the Baths of Diocletian (p. 106–107) some of the ancient interiors, still in fair condition, and the buildings that surround the cloister of Michelangelo contain exhibits ordered by the following themes: the city's foundation and early development; figurative at in the republican period; art and social class; the history of the Latin language and writing. In the Crypta Balbi a new display is being prepared on the early Middle Ages.

In the central archaeological precinct there is the new Museo Palatino (pp. 38–39) and the Antiquarium Forense, which contains archaeological remains found in the Forum, including the famous frieze from the Basilica Aemila.

A small collection of ancient sculptures, mostly Roman, is in the Museo Barracco on Corso Vittorio Emanuele.

A very different kind of collection, above all interesting for educational purposes, is the Museo della Civiltà Romana, housed in an imposing edifice in the EUR district. Its exhibits are almost exclusively reproductions which illustrate the history of the ancient nucleus of the city and various aspects of Roman civilisation. The exhibits are arranged chronologically. Of special interest is the model designed by the architect Italo Gismondi for the Mostra Augustea della Romanità (1937). The model covers about 200 square metres (on a scale of 1:250) and reproduces the city in the age of Constantine.

283 ▼   284 ▶

283. *The Capitoline She-Wolf. Etruscan bronze, early fifth century BC. The twins, Romulus and Remus, were probably added in the fifteenth century. Musei Capitolini, Rome.*
284. *A gallery of Roman sculpture from the age of Augustus in a painting by Lawrence Alma-Tadema (1867). Musée des Beaux-Arts, Montreal.*

THE MUSEI CAPITOLINI

This is the oldest public collection of ancient artworks in the world. Founded in 1471 by Pope Sixtus IV, it was opened to the public by Clement XII in the early eighteenth century. The collections of the Musei Capitolini, now owned by the city of Rome, include some outstandingly famous and important pieces, like the *Capitoline She-Wolf* (ill. 283). Some of the sculptures and other exhibits—many now displayed for the first time, like the statues from the pediment of the Temple of Apollo Sosianus (pp. 80–81)—are exhibited temporarily in rather unusual premises at the Centrale Montemartini on the Via Ostiense, the city's first thermo-electric power station. Today ancient relics are on display alongside early twentieth-century industrial machinery.

A particularly important exhibit in the Capitoline collections is the equestrian statue of Marcus Aurelius. This is one of the few bronze statues that has survived intact from ancient times. The decision not to melt it down for the sake of the bronze was probably due to the mistaken identification of the figure as Constantine, an emperor greatly revered in the Middle Ages because he was believed to have embraced Christianity. The statue of Marcus Aurelius on horseback almost certainly commemorates the triumph he was awarded for his victory over the Parthians, celebrated in Rome in 166 AD. At present the statue is on display in the museum where it was moved after restoration in the 1980s.

The statue was long kept in the Basilica of San Giovanni in Laterano; then, at the Renaissance, it was moved to the Piazza del Campidgolio (on the Capitol).

285 ◄   286 ▲

130

285. *Man in a Toga, the proud symbol of Roman citizenship imposed by Augustus, with images of his ancestors (50–40 BC). Centrale Montemartini, Rome.*
286. *Piazza del Campidoglio with Palazzo Nuovo (left) and Palazzo dei Conservatori (right), which house the Musei Capitolini.*
287. *Boy removing a thorn from his foot, bronze from the first century BC.*
288. *Equestrian statue of Marcus Aurelius, bronze from the second century AD. Musei Capitolini, Rome.*
289. *The Esquiline Venus, a sculpture associated with the cult of Isis, from the first century BC. Centrale Montemartini, Rome.*

288 ◄

289 ►

THE VATICAN MUSEUMS

The Vatican Museums and the Papal Galleries (Gallerie Pontifiche del Vaticano) form an outstandingly important museum complex by both the richness of their exhibits and the splendid setting. The holdings in the Museo Pio-Clementino, Museo Chiaramonti, Braccio Nuovo, Museo Egizio, and Museo Etrusco together form the world's largest collection of ancient art. The beginnings go back to the Renaissance popes, who displayed the nucleus of the collection in the Belvedere Courtyard. The original collection was depleted by gifts from the popes to the city of Rome and foreign sovereigns. The museum was reorganised by the popes of the eighteenth and nineteenth centuries.

The Vatican Museums contain many outstandingly important and famous works, including the *Laocoön* (ill. 293), the base of the Column of Antoninus Pius, two porphyry sarcophagi of St. Helena and Constantia, respectively mother and daughter of the Emperor Constantine, the *Apollo Belvedere*, the statue of Augustus from Prima Porta, and many others. There are also extensive Etruscan remains, including the furnishings of the Regolini-Galassi tomb and the bronze statue of the Mars of Todi.

290 ◀

291 ▶

290. *The Apoxyomenos, Roman copy (first century AD) of a Greek original by the sculptor Lysippus (circa 320 BC).*
291. *The Apollo Belvedere, copy of a Greek original of the fourth century BC.*
292. *View of the Braccio Nuovo in the Vatican Museums.*
293. *The Laocoön, exhibited in a niche of the Belvedere Courtyard. Vatican Museums, Rome.*
294. *Tiberius as Emperor (early first century AD).*

292 ▲ 293 ▼ 294 ▶

LA 2

PALAZZO MASSIMO
ALLE TERME

The collection at Palazzo Massimo alle Terme forms part of the Museo Nazionale Romano. It mainly displays material from the splendid houses of the senatorial class in Rome. These works, when viewed together with the items from the imperial palaces displayed at the Museo Palatino (pp. 38–39), provide a comprehensive panorama of the art of late republican and imperial Rome.

The second floor of the palace is wholly devoted to a display of the most significant examples of Roman decorative painting and mosaic pavements found in Rome and Lazio, including some recent discoveries.

The display includes reconstructions of some interiors of important residential complexes, such as Livia's villa at Prima Porta and the Villa della Farnesina on Via della Lungara. In particular the reconstruction of some interiors with the frescoes on the walls and stuccoed vaulting reveals the conceptual unity of the decoration, which is usually seen only as fragments.

MUSEUMS

295 ▲   296 ▶

295. *Battle between Dionysus and the Indians, from Villa della Ruffinella, mosaic of the earlier fourth century AD.*
296. *Frescoes in Livia's villa at Prima Porta; detail of the garden paintings from the triclinium.*

297 ▲   298 ▼

297. *Frescoes from the Villa della Farnesina: alcove wall with, in the central panel, the infant Dionysus, Leucothea and the nymphs of Nysa.*
298. *Mosaic with a cat and ducks, from a Roman villa on the Via Ardeatina (early first century BC).*

The ground floor of Palazzo Massimo contains examples of iconography and portraiture from the late republican period, with a display of sculptural decorations from the residences of the wealthy classes. Many statues are Roman copies of Greek originals by great sculptors such as Lysippus and Praxiteles (both fourth century BC).

The basement level has sections devoted to numismatics—covering ancient times, the Middle Ages and the present—and a display of jewels and household items made of precious materials, mostly from imperial times. The artefacts mostly come from tombs regularly excavated, so the objects can be dated and understood in their cultural and historical setting and not viewed merely as collectors' pieces. Among the exhibits is an unusual example of the embalmed body of a little girl with her tomb furnishings from Grottarossa (second century BC).

299 ▲
300 ▼

301 ▶

302 ▶

303 ▶

304 ▲

305 ▼

306 ▶

137

PALAZZO ALTEMPS

In the second half of the sixteenth century Cardinal Altemps decided to transform the family palace, under construction for a century, into "a home for statues." Subsequently, however, the cardinal's collection of ancient sculptures and his rich library were dispersed, a destiny shared by the majority of the patrician collections, which frequently changed hands.

The building has recently been restructured by Rome's Soprintendenza Archeologica to recreate the original Cinquecento interior. It now contains sixteen sculptures that once belonged to the Altemps collection and items from other important collections, like the Boncompagni Ludovisi and Mattei collections and the Egyptian collection of the Museo Nazionale Romano. The antiquarian reconstruction of the original Cinquecento setting was suggested by the close relations between the Ludovisi and Altemps collections, with pieces passing between the two families. Restoration of the interiors now enables visitors to admire the splendid statues at the same time as they view the magnificent building that houses them.

307 ▲   308 ▼   309 ▶

307. *The Ludovisi Throne, depicting the birth of Aphrodite Urania, from the fifth century BC.*
308. *The Ludovisi Altar: Roman copy of an original of the Hellenistic period.*
309. *The loggia of Palazzo Altemps with portraits of the Caesars from the Ludovisi collection.*
310. *Ancient carving in red marble with the mask of Dionysus, from the decoration of a fountain.*
311. *The Suicide of Galatea from the Ludovisi collection. It has recently been suggested that this statue and the Death of Galatea (now in the Musei Capitolini) both stood in the octagonal chamber of the Domus Aurea.*

310 ▲   311 ▼

The Emperors of Rome

EMPEROR	REIGN
Augustus (in the photo)	27 BC–14 AD
Tiberius	14–37
Caligula	37–41
Claudius	41–54
Nero	54–68
Galba	68–69
Otho	69
Vitellius	69
Vespasian	69–79
Titus	79–81
Domitian	81–96
Nerva	96–98
Trajan	98–117
Hadrian	117–138
Antoninus Pius	138–161
Marcus Aurelius	161–180
Commodus	180–192
Pertinax	193
Didius Iulianus	193
Septimius Severus	193–211
Caracalla	198–217
Geta	209–212
Macrinus	217–218
Heliogabalus	218–22
Alexander Severus	222–235
Maximinus	235–238
Gordian I	238
Gordian II	238
Pupienus	238
Balbinus	238
Gordian III	238–244
Philip	244–249
Decius	248–251
Gallus	251–253
Aemilianus	253
Valerian	253–260
Gallienus	253–268
Postumus	260–268
Lelianus	268
Marius	268
Victorinus	268–270
Claudius II	268–270
Tetricus	270–274
Aurelian	270–275
Tacitus	275–276
Probus	276–282
Carus (Carinus and Numerian)	282–285
Diocletian	284–305
Maximinian	286–305
Constantius Chlorus	305–306
Galerius	305–311
Flavius Severus	306–307
Maxentius	306–312
Maximin Daza	308–313
Constantine I (the Great)	306–337
Licinius	308–323
Constantine II	337–340
Constans	307–350
Constantius	337–361
Magnentius	350-353
Julian	361–363
Jovian	363–364
Valentinian I	364–375
Valens	364–378
Gratian	367–383
Valentinian II	375–392
Theodosius	379–395
Honorius	395–423
John	423–425
Valentinian III	425–455
Maximus	455
Avitus	455–456
Majorian	457–461
Libius Severus	461–465
Anthemius	467–472
Olybrius	472
Glycerius	473–474
Julius Nepos	474–475
Romulus Augustulus	475–476

Index

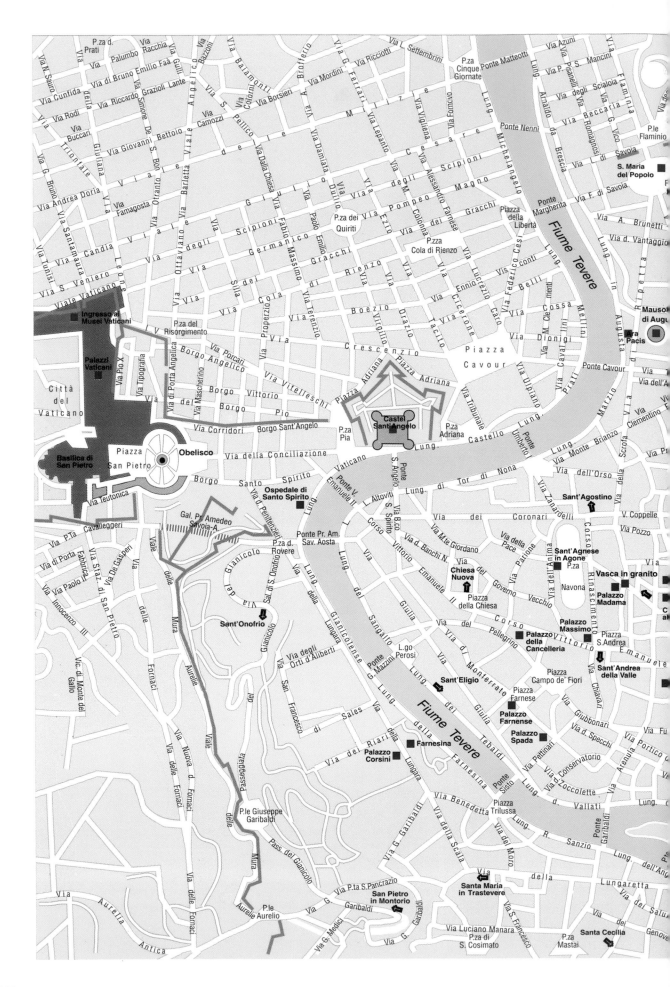

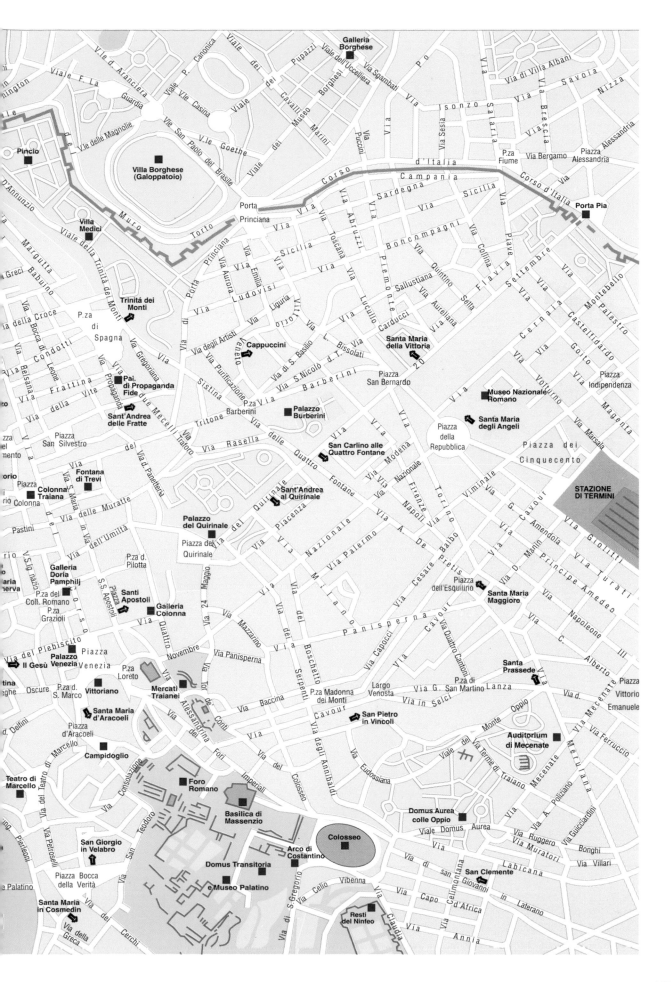

Galleria
Borghese

Pincio

Villa Borghese
(Galoppatoio)

Porta Pia

Villa
Medici

Porta
Princiana

Trinitá dei
Monti

P.za
di
Spagna

Santa Maria
della Vittoria

Cappuccini

Museo Nazionale
Romano

Pai.
di Propaganda
Fide

Palazzo
Burberini

Santa Maria
degli Angeli

Sant'Andrea
delle Fratte

Piazza
San Silvestro

San Carlino alle
Quattro Fontane

Piazza
della
Repubblica

Piazza dei
Cinquecento

STAZIONE
DI TERMINI

Fontana
di Trevi

Sant'Andrea
al Quirinale

Colonna
Traiana

Palazzo
del Quirinale

Piazza del
Quirinale

Galleria
Doria
Pamphilj

P.za d.
Pilotta

Santi
Apostoli

Piazza
dell'Esquilino

Santa Maria
Maggiore

P.za del
Coll. Romano

Galleria
Colonna

P.za
Grazioli

Palazzo
Venezia

Il Gesú

Piazza
Venezia

P.za
Loreto

Santa
Prassede

P.za di
San Martino

Vittorio
Emanuele

P.za d.
S. Marco

Vittoriano

Mercati
Traianei

P.za Madonna
dei Monti

Largo
Venosta

Santa Maria
d'Aracoeli

San Pietro
in Vincoli

Piazza
d'Aracoeli

Auditorium
di Mecenate

Campidoglio

Teatro di
Marcello

Foro
Romano

Domus Aurea
colle Oppio

Basilica di
Massenzio

San Giorgio
in Velabro

Colosseo

Arco di
Costantino

San Clemente

Domus Transitoria

Piazza Bocca
della Veritá

e Museo Palatino

Santa Maria
in Cosmedin

Resti
del Ninfeo

143

Translation by
Richard Sadleir

www.electaweb.it

Reprint 2010
First Edition 2000

This book was printed on behalf of Mondadori Electa S.p.A.
at Mondadori Printing S.p.A., Verona, in the year 2010